ONTARIO
WINE
COUNTRY

ONTARIO WINE COUNTRY

text **Rod Phillips**   photography **Lorraine Parow**

whitecap

Edited by Elizabeth Wilson
Proofread by Marilyn Bittman and Ben D'Andrea
Cover design by Jane Lightle and Five Seventeen
Interior design by Margaret Lee/bamboosilk.com
Typeset by Jacqui Thomas and Five Seventeen
Map by Eric Leinberger

Printed and bound in Canada

Library and Archives Canada Cataloguing in Publication
Phillips, Roderick
      Ontario wine country / Rod Phillips.

Includes index.
ISBN 1-55285-649-6

      1. Wineries—Ontario—Guidebooks. 2. Wine and wine
making—Ontario. I. Title.

TP559.C3P55 2006   663'.2'009713   C2005-906782-9

The publisher acknowledges the support of the Canada Council and the Cultural
Services Branch of the Government of British Columbia in making this publication
possible. We acknowledge the financial support of the Government of Canada through
the Book Publishing Industry Development Program for our publishing activities.

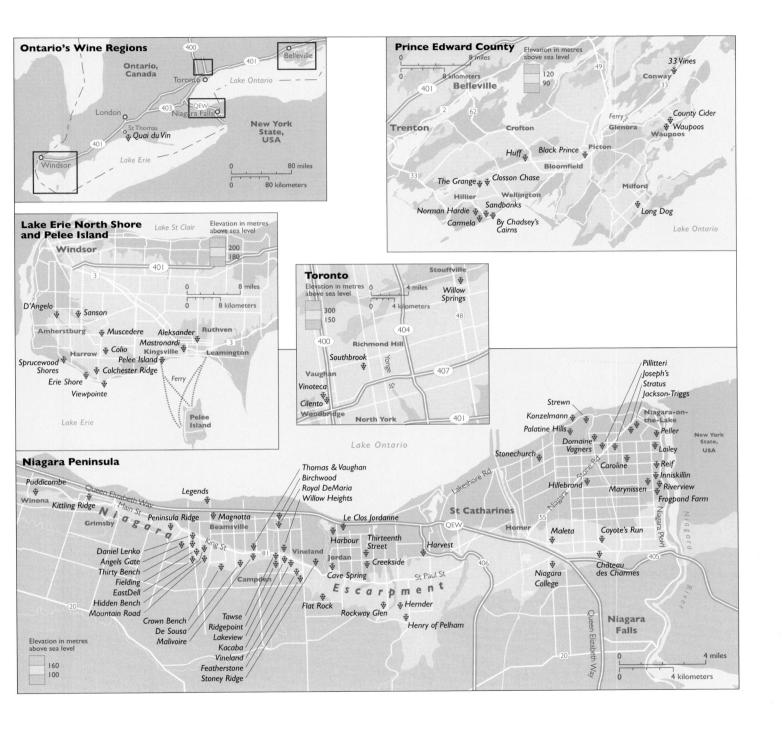

Ontario's Wine Regions

400
401
Belleville
Ontario, Canada
Toronto
Lake Ontario
London
403
QEW
Niagara Falls
St Thomas
Quai du Vin
New York State, USA
401
Windsor
Lake Erie
80 miles
80 kilometers

Prince Edward County

8 miles
Elevation in metres above sea level
120
90
8 kilometers
401
49
33 Vines
Conway
33
2
62
Belleville
Ferry
County Cider
Trenton
Crofton
Glenora
Waupoos
Waupoos
Huff
Black Prince
Picton
Bloomfield
33
The Grange
Closson Chase
Milford
Hillier
Wellington
Norman Hardie
Sandbanks
Carmela
By Chadsey's Cairns
Long Dog
Lake Ontario

Lake Erie North Shore and Pelee Island

Lake St Clair
Elevation in metres above sea level
200
180
Windsor
401
3
8 miles
8 kilometers
D'Angelo
Sanson
Amherstburg
Muscedere
Aleksander
Ruthven
Mastronardi
3
Colio
Kingsville
Leamington
Harrow
Pelee Island
Sprucewood Shores
Colchester Ridge
Erie Shore
Viewpointe
Ferry
Lake Erie
Pelee Island

Toronto

Stouffville
Elevation in metres above sea level
4 miles
Willow Springs
4 kilometers
48
404
400
Richmond Hill
407
Southbrook
Yonge St
Vaughan
Vinoteca
Cilento
401
Woodbridge
North York

Niagara Peninsula

Puddicombe
Winona
Kittling Ridge
Queen Elizabeth Way
Main St
Legends
Thomas & Vaughan
Birchwood
Royal DeMaria
Willow Heights
Pillitteri
Joseph's
Stratus
Jackson-Triggs
Grimsby
Niagara
Peninsula Ridge
Magnotta
Beamsville
Strewn
Konzelmann
Niagara-on-the-Lake
Peller
King St
Le Clos Jordanne
Palatine Hills
Domaine Vagners
Lailey
New York State, USA
Daniel Lenko
Angels Gate
Thirty Bench
Fielding
EastDell
Hidden Bench
Mountain Road
81
Vineland
Harbour
Thirteenth Street
Jordan
Creekside
Cave Spring
Harvest
Stonechurch
Caroline
Reif
Hillebrand
Marynissen
Inniskillin
Riverview
Frogpond Farm
St Catharines
Homer
55
Maleta
Coyote's Run
Lakeshore Rd
Niagara Stone Rd
Niagara Pkwy
20
Campden
Crown Bench
De Sousa
Malivoire
Tawse
Ridgepoint
Lakeview
Kacaba
Vineland
Featherstone
Stoney Ridge
Flat Rock
Rockway Glen
St Paul St
Hernder
Henry of Pelham
Escarpment
Niagara College
406
Chateau des Charmes
405
Niagara River
Elevation in metres above sea level
160
100
20
Queen Elizabeth Way
Niagara Falls
4 miles
4 kilometers
Lake Ontario

ACKNOWLEDGMENTS

The most important acknowledgment is a collective one. Throughout Ontario's wine regions, winemakers, owners, vineyard managers, communications people, tasting bar staff, and others took the time and trouble to show me around, answer my questions, and pour me their wines. Some of their names, stories, and insights punctuate the text, but the rest are in my notes and memory. They made the research and writing of this book an almost undiluted pleasure.

In each region, key people gave practical assistance. Laurie McDonald of Vintners Quality Alliance Ontario (VQA) kept me up to date with the sub-appellations. Rebecca LeHeup-Bucknell and Grace Nyman of Taste the County set up visits to Prince Edward County. Sandra Bradt, Director of Tourism at the Convention and Visitors Bureau of Windsor, and Judy Insley of Great Events International, not only organized a visit to Lake Erie North Shore and Pelee Island, but accompanied me throughout.

In Ottawa, friends and colleagues helped out in myriad ways. Cynthia Mar did everything from sorting out my occasional computer problems to reading through parts of the manuscript. Janet Dorozynski was always ready to talk and taste Ontario wine, and she also read parts of the manuscript. Vic Harradine, my friend and partner in winecurrent.com, read some of the text and took on extra wine reviews to give me time to tie up loose ends on this book.

Finally, it has been a pleasure to work with Lorraine Parow, whose images enhance my words, and Allison McLean and AnnMarie McKinnon at Whitecap Books. Elizabeth Wilson has been one of the easiest editors I've worked with.

No doubt, errors will have found their way into the text ("What do you mean, their first Syrah was 2001? I have a bottle of their 2000 in my cellar!") but they should be few. I offered every winery the opportunity to check its entry for factual errors and all but two signed off on the accuracy, if not the tone, of my commentary. Still, I take final responsibility for any factual errors that might have crept in.

— ROD PHILLIPS
OTTAWA, DECEMBER 2005

CONTENTS

INTRODUCTION

It's easy to forget how young Ontario's wine industry is. Wine has been made commercially in the province for a century and a half, and some present-day wineries can trace their lineage back to the beginnings. But two-thirds of Ontario's wineries have opened since 1999. Even in the Niagara Peninsula, the most established of Ontario's wine regions, more than half have opened since that year.

The sheer newness of it all was brought home to me in 2004, when I was talking to Jean-Pierre Colas, winemaker at Peninsula Ridge Estate in Beamsville, and tasting his latest vintage. He said he'd like to come to Ottawa to do a vertical tasting to show how his wines had evolved. This seemed a good idea, but as I started nodding, a thought struck me, and I said, "But you've only been making wine here since 2000. Your vertical would only cover four vintages."

He knew that, of course, but what struck me at the time was how much a fixture on Ontario's wine landscape Peninsula Ridge already felt. It seemed I'd been drinking their wine for many more years than four, and this was true of many Ontario wineries that had opened at about the same time.

Ontario's wineries—and therefore the wine region itself—are still in the early phases of development. Many are still finding their feet, trying to decide on the varieties that do best in their vineyards, working out the relationships between their grapes and methods of vinification, their wines, and barrels. Winemaking is always a journey like this—and vintage variation ensures that no one can ever be complacent and adopt a rigid recipe—but in the early years, everything is that much less certain.

The picture keeps changing. In the year I finished writing this book, no fewer than ten wineries opened and others merged or changed hands, while a dozen or so winemakers moved from one winery to another, left Ontario, or arrived from countries as diverse as Australia and Romania. Interviews I had written up had to be done again and text revised. Writing a book like this is like painting a bridge: by the time you finish, the first bit has to be re-done.

Yet co-existing with the flux of early development, Ontario has also established its shape as a maturing wine region that produces excellent wines. The sheer quality of much of the wine produced by Ontario wineries in the last five to ten years has overcome the prejudices that middle-aged wine-drinkers carried from their youthful forays into cheap Ontario wine. Meanwhile, younger generations, travelling without the same prejudice-packed baggage, have begun to appreciate the province's wine.

Establishing a reputation and market in Canada is critical for Ontario's wines, but international recognition (and markets) are important, too. Icewine has created a beachhead among foreign wine-lovers, and Ontario table wines will follow before long.

What I've tried to do here is provide a snapshot of the wine regions and their wineries, owners, and winemakers at this dynamic phase of Ontario's emergence as a participant in the new world of wine. This book documents the paths that regions and wineries have taken, and in many cases reveals the winemaker, as much as the grapes, in the bottle.

OPPOSITE: **AGING VINES IN A MATURING WINE REGION**

WINE IN ONTARIO, PAST AND PRESENT

THE WINDS OF CHANGE THAT BEGAN TO RUSTLE THE LEAVES IN VINEYARDS AROUND THE WORLD STIRRED THE FOLIAGE IN ONTARIO, TOO.

THE BEGINNINGS

The early history of wine in Ontario is very murky, just as the early wine itself undoubtedly was. Although grapes grow wild in many parts of the province, there's no evidence that native peoples ever fermented them to make wine. Like beer and spirits, wine made its way to North America as European settlers brought small amounts for use in religious services and more substantial volumes for daily consumption. But it was expensive and difficult to ship wine across the Atlantic, and much of it must have reached its destination in an undrinkable state. What arrived in potable condition (and probably what didn't, too) was expensive and was therefore consumed only by the better off.

Quite possibly, some of the new Canadian gentry tried making wine from the locally available grapes. There are no records of anyone trying to make table wine from labrusca grapes, the main species that grew wild in North America, but French priests in Québec tried fermenting them to make sacramental wine in the 1600s. They soon abandoned the experiment. Communion wine was sipped only by the priest in those days, but it seems that even that small amount of wine made from the inferior native grapes was too much.

OPPOSITE: **A PLACE IN THE VINEYARD TO SIT AND DRINK**

13

We do know that some Europeans who settled in the Niagara Peninsula in the late 1700s planted grapevines, but we don't know for sure whether they ate them as fresh fruit, preserved them, or used them to make wine. By that time, wine was made in several northeastern states, where many of Ontario's early settlers came from. They might well have brought their vine-growing and winemaking skills to Upper Canada (as Ontario was known), where the climate was far more favourable to viticulture. But even if they did make wine, it wasn't on a commercial basis, for the great majority of settlers in eastern Canada took their daily alcohol in the form of beer and spirits, like rum and whisky.

ONTARIO'S EARLIEST WINERIES

Not until the early 1800s can we identify someone who produced wine in Ontario. In 1811, Johann Schiller, a German immigrant, made wine in what is now the Mississauga area of Toronto. Not a lot is known about Schiller. He's variously described as a "German mercenary," a "retired German corporal," and "a German soldier." Some accounts say he gathered wild grapes from the banks of the Credit River, some that he planted a vineyard with indigenous vines, others that he cultivated hybrid varieties. He's said to have sold his wine to his neighbours, but that doesn't mean he was a commercial winemaker: the sale and exchange of home-grown produce among neighbours was common in those days. Moreover, Schiller's garagiste operation seems to have had a short life, and there's no record of the wine's style or quality.

Schiller is too insubstantial a figure to wear the "Father of Ontario Wine" title he's often given, because there's absolutely no evidence he was a model or inspiration to others. That might say something about the quality of his wine. Still, unless evidence of other winemakers comes to light, he's certainly the first in the province to be identified by name.

The next two records of wine production in Ontario date from 1864, which strongly suggests that we're missing a lot of history; it's unlikely that no wine was made in Ontario for 50 years. The first reference relates to a Vine Growers' Association set up by Count Justin de Courtenay in 1864. De Courtenay wrote two pamphlets on viticulture and winemaking, and founded the Château Clair winery, which is said to have made sparkling, white, and red wines. Some were exhibited at the 1867 Paris Exposition, where they were apparently well received. Without wanting to detract too much from de Courtenay's achievement, we should note that many American wines also did well in Paris in 1867.

De Courtenay planned for substantial production. Château Clair's cellars are said to have had a capacity for 20,000 gallons, the equivalent of 10,000 cases of wine, far more than the annual production of many modern Ontario wineries. But Château Clair didn't survive. It was followed by wineries that experienced varying degrees of success.

The second reference to winemaking in 1864 comes from Prince Edward County, at the eastern end of Lake Ontario's north shore. An advertisement in a Toronto magazine announced that J.H. Morden and Son were "manufacturing a pure grape wine, from Grapes grown on their own premises." It was described, in terms forbidden to producers today, as "superior for Medicinal Purposes to the adulterated and drugged mixtures daily exposed for sale," "highly recommended by the best judges in Canada," and "very suitable for sacramental purposes."

In fact, the 1860s seem to have been a boom period for wine throughout Ontario. In 1866, the year before Confederation, Thaddeus Smith and two other Kentucky entrepreneurs planted about 25 acres (10 hectares) of labrusca vines on Pelee Island, in Lake Erie, and established the Vin Villa winery. Starting with their first vintage, in 1871, they sold some grapes to wineries across the lake in Ohio and also made wine and sold it in Ontario. A little later, in 1873, George Barnes set up a winery on the Niagara Peninsula, near St. Catharines, and the following year, T.G. Bright opened a winery, bearing his name, near Niagara Falls. Both proved to be enduring and important wineries.

About the same time, Dorland Noxon planted vines in Hillier Township in Prince Edward County. The varieties he planted aren't known, but one of his wines won a medal at the 1876 Centennial Exhibition in Philadelphia. In 1888, J.S. Hamilton founded the Pelee Island Wine and Vineyard Company wineries on Pelee Island and in Brantford, and by 1894 he was making what might have been Canada's first sparkling wine. It was sold under the grand name L'Empereur Champagne. Other wineries planted vineyards and opened their doors at this time, but little is known about many of them.

By 1900, Ontario's vineyards covered some 11,250 acres (4,500 hectares), which is about two-thirds the area of land under vines in the province today. There were probably about three dozen wineries in Niagara. On the north shore of Lake Erie and on Pelee Island, there were perhaps two dozen more, but their number declined in the early 1900s, partly because tobacco became a more lucrative crop than grapes. Prince Edward County's fledgling industry was stifled when, in the era of Prohibition, the district went dry.

These turn-of-the-century wineries varied in size and longevity, but all shared an initial reliance on North American labrusca grape varieties. Attempts to grow Vitis vinifera, the classic European varieties such as Chardonnay and Merlot, failed when the vines succumbed to pests, phylloxera, diseases, or to Ontario winters. Native varieties were the best bet simply because of their proven ability to survive.

The best-known labrusca grape was Concord, which had been cultivated in New York in the 1840s. It quickly became the mainstay of Ontario vineyards, used for both grape juice (which was made commercially from the late 1800s) and wine. Other native varieties included Catawba, Niagara, and Elvira. Labrusca grapes made only mediocre wine, and most of the wine produced was fortified with brandy and made in styles that were likened to

**CORKS FROM HARBOUR ESTATES WINERY,
A YOUNG NIAGARA PRODUCER**

GRAPE SEEDS SEPARATED FROM SKIN AND JUICE

either port or sherry. Table wine was only a small part of production, perhaps a fifth at most.

In the late 1800s and early 1900s, Ontario consumers could buy wine directly from wineries and from general stores. Before the advent of Ontario's provincially run beverage alcohol system, the Liquor Control Board of Ontario (the LCBO, founded in 1927), wine was generally sold in bulk, along with food and other provisions.

PROHIBITION

The LCBO maintains its dominant position in the sale of beverage alcohol in Ontario today partly because of fear of unrestrained access to alcohol, the very fear that gave rise to a movement against alcohol in the late 1800s. Powerful temperance and prohibition movements emerged in North America, Australasia, Great Britain, and in some parts of Europe, like Scandinavia. Many countries introduced restrictions on the sale of alcohol, such as setting minimum drinking ages. But few went as far as the United States, where state after state banned the production and sale of alcohol, and where nation-wide Prohibition was eventually introduced by an amendment to the Constitution in 1919.

In Canada, various restrictions were placed on the production and sale of alcohol, but it wasn't until the First World War that the provinces began to introduce Prohibition. Governments were less concerned about the morality of drinking than preserving resources for war-related needs and improving productivity by reducing drinking and drunkenness. But in Ontario, locally produced wine was given a qualified exemption from Prohibition.

Beer and spirit sales were banned, but wine made in the province could be sold from wineries in minimum volumes of five gallons (about 30 standard bottles). Wine could also be obtained for medical and religious purposes.

These exemptions reflected distinctions made between wine and other beverage alcohol in temperance and prohibition legislation elsewhere. Wine was regarded as "natural," while spirits were "industrial." Wine also benefited from a long association with religion and good health. Favoured by the upper classes, wine was associated with civility, whereas beer and spirits were the drinks of the unruly working classes.

From 1916, when the Ontario version of Prohibition came into force, wine was the only alcoholic drink legally available in the province and, not surprisingly, the wine industry prospered. Dozens of new wineries opened in Niagara and along the north shore of Lake Erie, as well as in less likely locations throughout the province. Between 1916 and 1927, the era of Prohibition in Ontario, the number of wineries grew from about a dozen to between 40 and 50. Sales of wine shot up—a hundredfold, according to some accounts—but it's generally agreed that the wine was worse than any made before or since in the province. Quality was clearly not an issue when wine was the only available beverage that contained alcohol.

FROM LABRUSCA VINES TO HYBRIDS

Although winery owners profited from this Prohibition-era boom, it set Ontario's wine industry back over the long term. As soon as beer and spirits came back on stream, demand for wine ebbed, and the memory of the period's ghastly products not only soured a generation on Ontario wine but became a cultural memory in the province. Many wineries deservedly went bankrupt and the provincial authorities refused to issue new winery licences for the next 50 years, partly because of the experience of the 1920s. Finally, as Prohibition ended, the government established the Liquor Control Board of Ontario, which, for all its merits, has generally impeded the ability of Ontario wineries to sell their products.

The much-reduced industry made important changes between the 1930s and 1950s. One was the search for French hybrid varieties that could survive Ontario winters and make better wine than could be coaxed from labrusca grapes. Of the dozens of hybrid varieties tried, several were chosen as most suitable for the Niagara Peninsula region and, during the 1950s and 1960s, varieties like Baco Noir, Seyval Blanc, Vidal, and Maréchal Foch began to dominate Ontario's vineyards.

The maturation of these hybrid wines coincided with the renewed wine interest of the 1960s and 1970s. Although most of Ontario's wine was still sherry and port styles, new brands of table wine came onto the market. Some were labelled with European names and wine regions, like Burgundy, Chablis, Beaujolais, Champagne, the Rhine, and Sauternes. Producers wooed sophisticated drinkers by offering them wines with European names like Alpenweiss, Toscano, Sommet Blanc, Côte Ste. Catherine Vin Rouge, and Wunderbar.

Ontario wine law at that time was so lax that hybrid varieties could be used to make wine that was then labelled as vinifera. For example, Château Cartier Canadian Riesling was made predominantly from Delaware, a hybrid developed in New York. And needless to say, wines named after French appellations were not made from the varieties grown there. Brights President Burgundy was made from Maréchal Foch (not Pinot Noir) and Barnes Sauternes was made from Elvira and Niagara (not Sauvignon Blanc or Semillon).

Other wines from the '60s and '70s appealed to the new hip market of baby boomers, who started to reach drinking age (then 21) in 1967. Producers began to market wines with far-out names like Lonesome Charlie, Baby Bear, and Gimli Goose. There was even a cola-flavoured wine called Zoom, but the bestseller was a sparkling wine called Baby Duck. Ironically, it was made from Concord, a labrusca variety. What were these wines like? John Reid's 1975 guide to Canadian wines in the LCBO was quite complimentary about the reds, but struggled with the whites: "When it's fresh, it's pleasant,"

"Despite what connoisseurs might call a bland character, it's satisfying in a quiet way," and "rather caramelly, soft with an undistinguished flavour."

These wines are now regarded with some scorn, and among many wine lovers Baby Duck, which is still produced, is a byword for mediocre Ontario wine. But such wines marked an important phase in the development of both the Ontario wine industry and Ontario's wine consumers. Their quality was undoubtedly low when compared to today's Ontario wines, but they were a big improvement on the labrusca-based, sugared-up concoctions that had dominated the market until the 1960s. And the use of superior hybrid varieties, which didn't have to be disguised by brandy and other additives, allowed producers to pay more attention to making table wines more suitable for drinking with meals.

OPPOSITE: **OVERSEEING THE FRUIT OF THEIR YEAR'S WORK**

BELOW: **READY FOR THE CRUSH**

THE QUALITY REVOLUTION

A global revolution in wine began in the 1970s. Countries that had made mainly mediocre wine for decades and even centuries—New Zealand, Australia, South Africa, Chile, and the United States—began to produce quality wine that could compete on world markets. So did many parts of Europe—like southern France, southern Italy, and Spain—that had historically produced plonk for local consumers.

The winds of change that began to rustle the leaves in vineyards around the world stirred the foliage in Ontario, too. Even though hybrids were doing well, there was renewed interest in vinifera varieties, and Brights, Château Cartier, and Château-Gai had all planted parcels of vinifera in the 1950s and 1960s. Brights had a large block of Chardonnay, and released Ontario's first varietal Chardonnay in 1956. Château Cartier and Château-Gai planted Gamay, and their 1973 "Gamay Beaujolais" was sold by the

LCBO. In 1975, critic John Reid wrote that they "are to be commended for attempting to grow the sensitive vinifera grape in our adverse conditions—and both resulting wines are worth trying. In flavour they're similarly light-bodied and refreshingly clean and savoury—although they don't taste much like

LOOKING UP THE BENCH AT PENINSULA RIDGE ESTATES WINERY

Gamays from France. Drink the '73s now."

During the 1970s and 1980s, plantings of vinifera increased. In 1976, vinifera accounted for 1.6 percent of all the vines in Ontario, but by 1981 they represented 5.6 percent, and by 1986 they made up 9.5 percent. The number of vinifera vines increased 500 percent between 1976 and 1986, while hybrids grew by only 85 percent, and native vines (still the vast majority) declined by three percent. The biggest gains were made by Riesling and Chardonnay, but Gamay, Pinot Noir, and Gewürztraminer started to take hold.

An important development was the appearance of new wineries dedicated to vinifera. The first was Inniskillin, now one of Ontario's best-known wineries. In 1974, Donald Ziraldo, who ran a family nursery in Niagara, was granted a licence to make

500 gallons of Gamay for submission to the LCBO. The following year, he and his partner, amateur winemaker Karl Kaiser, founded Inniskillin Wines. Inniskillin was soon followed by others. Paul Bosc established Château des Charmes in 1978, and planted the first 100 percent vinifera vineyard, on St. David's Bench. Bosc was convinced that the climate and soil were similar enough to Burgundy to plant mainly Chardonnay and Pinot Noir (the Burgundy varieties) on his 50-acre (20-hectare) property. Château des Charmes' vineyards were so significant that by 1981 its vines accounted for 20 percent of all the vinifera growing in Ontario.

Between 1975 and the late-1980s, several more wineries opened. They included Newark (now Hillebrand), Colio Estate, the first incarnation of Stoney Ridge (located on the site of the present Puddicombe Farms Estate), Pelee Island Winery, St. Urbanshof (the precursor of Vineland Estates), Reif Estates, Konzelmann Estate, and Henry of Pelham Family Estate Winery. At the same time, many independent grape growers began to plant vinifera and sell the fruit to wineries.

One of this period's innovations, which no one imagined would become so important to Ontario's wine industry, was icewine, which is made by allowing grapes to hang on the vine until they shrivel and then eventually freeze. They're picked and pressed frozen, to extract the tiny amount of sugar-filled juice, which has a higher freezing point than water. The sweet, viscous juice is then fermented into an ultra-sweet, intensely flavoured dessert wine.

Icewine has been made since the 1700s in Germany, Austria, and Switzerland. The first commercial Canadian icewine was made in 1978 in the Okanagan valley by a German immigrant, Walter Hainle. In the early 1980s, several Ontario winemakers realized that Ontario has ideal winter conditions for icewine. A number of wineries, including Hillebrand Estate and Pelee Island, produced icewine in 1983, and Karl Kaiser started making icewine at Inniskillin in 1984. (The birds got to Kaiser's 1983 crop before he did.) Before long, icewine production put Canada on the world wine map.

FREE TRADE AND THE VQA

Just as Ontario's wine industry seemed to be taking off in the 1980s with new wineries, vineyards newly planted with vinifera, and the new icewines, a new threat loomed. In 1989 the Canadian government entered into the North American Free Trade Agreement (NAFTA) with the United States. Together with other trade rules, it cut away at the preferential treatment and pricing of Canadian wines in provincial liquor stores. Ontario wines would have to compete on a level playing field with wines from California and elsewhere. Pessimists predicted the end of Ontario's wine industry, but in fact NAFTA accelerated the shift to quality. The Ontario government spent $50 million to compensate growers who pulled out inferior grape varieties, and between 1986 and 1991 Ontario lost 20 percent of its vines. Labrusca and hybrid varieties declined, and what remained of them was increasingly used for juice and jam. Vitis vinifera, on the other hand, increased its proportion of all vines from 10 to almost 25 percent. The government also provided wineries with forgivable loans to upgrade their equipment and facilities.

One sign that the industry itself was beginning to take quality seriously was the Vintners Quality Alliance (VQA). It was set up first in Ontario as a way of guaranteeing the appellation, grape variety, vintage, and quality of Ontario wines. Like many wine laws, VQA sets out the grape varieties that are approved, and the rules clearly reflected the sense that Ontario had to leave behind its history of making wine with inferior grapes. Vinifera varieties were specified, along with several superior hybrids, notably Baco Noir, Vidal, and Maréchal Foch. The VQA program began as a voluntary code of quality, but in 1999 the Ontario government enshrined the

THE CONTOURS OF NIAGARA'S VINESCAPE

rules in legislation, thus giving Ontario its first wine law. Since then, various changes have been made, including one that allows wineries to seal their VQA wines with a screw cap.

THE 1990s AND BEYOND

Armed with a wine law (albeit voluntary at first), a growing number and selection of vinifera varieties, and new wineries with ambitious new winemakers, Ontario's wine industry looked set to make big strides from the beginning of the 1990s. They were slowed at first by a sluggish economy that discouraged investment, but the decade started with a symbolic bang. In 1991, the Inniskillin 1989 Vidal Icewine won the top award, the Grand Prix d'Honneur, in the international competition at Vinexpo, France's most prestigious wine show.

Another twenty wineries opened in Ontario during the 1990s, and there were the first signs of concentration of ownership. In 1989, Donald Triggs, who had been a vice-president of Labatt, a brewer with wine holdings, assembled a consortium to buy one of Labatt's wine companies, Niagara's Cartier Wines. Three years later, Cartier merged with Inniskillin, and then in 1993 with Brights. Within five years, Triggs had created Canada's largest wine company. In 1994, he named it Vincor. Although Vincor is now the fourth largest wine company in North America, it's better known to Ontario consumers by the names of its constituent wineries, Inniskillin and Jackson-Triggs (Allan Jackson is one of Triggs's partners). Vincor's winery holdings now extend to British Columbia, California, Washington, Australia, New Zealand, and South Africa, and include a wine distribution network in the United Kingdom.

The transformations that took place in the 1990s began to show up on the General List of the LCBO. Instead of the labrusca and hybrid varieties that had dominated Ontario wines on the list 10 or 20 years earlier, by the mid-1990s there was a wide range of vinifera-based wines made in Ontario. By 1994, the LCBO General List included Ontario Riesling, Sauvignon Blanc, Chardonnay, Pinot Blanc, Pinot Gris, Gewürztraminer, Gamay, Pinot Noir, Cabernet Sauvignon, and Cabernet Franc. They were still outnumbered by Ontario wines with names like Alpenweiss, Botticelli, Chablis, Sauternes, Burgundy, and Toscano, but the vinous tide was turning.

Since the middle of the 1990s, a period during which the great majority of today's Ontario wineries began making wine, there have been several important lines of change. The most obvious has been the growing population of wineries. Two thirds of Ontario's wineries have opened since 1999. This is to be expected in an emerging region like Prince Edward County, where nearly all the wineries are new; but even in the long-established Niagara Peninsula, more than half of the wineries have opened since 1999 and the proliferation of producers makes it difficult for consumers to keep up with what's on offer.

The newcomers can be divided into two broad categories. Many are owned by former grape growers who decided to make their own wine. Examples are Daniel Lenko (Daniel Lenko Estate Winery), Steve Kocsis (Mountain Road Wine Company), and John Neufeld (Palatine Hills Estate Winery). Other new wineries have been founded by people who made their money in other careers and are passionate enough about wine to risk investing in vineyards and a winery. Recent examples are Moray Tawse (Tawse Winery) who is a mortgage financier, David Feldberg (Stratus Vineyards) who is CEO of an office furniture company, and Ken and Marg Fielding (Fielding Estate Winery) who were in the fast-food business.

A second change is the attention given to grape varieties. Scores of varieties, vinifera and hybrids, are used in the making of Ontario wines, but not all do equally well. There's general agreement that in the Niagara Peninsula, the most successful whites are Riesling, Chardonnay, and Sauvignon Blanc, and the best reds are Gamay, Pinot Noir, and Cabernet Franc. Yet some winemakers are less positive about Pinot Noir in the region. There's also disagreement about Syrah: some producers are planting acres of it, while others are holding back, still unconvinced about its future. There's some skepticism, too, about the future of Cabernet Sauvignon and Merlot. They can be very good when they ripen fully (as in 1998, 2001, and 2002), but many cool Ontario vintages leave them with unattractive green notes. In the other Ontario wine regions, different varieties predominate. In Lake Erie North Shore and Pelee Island, Cabernet Sauvignon, Cabernet Franc, and Merlot do very well. In Prince Edward County, the hopes are on Pinot Noir and Chardonnay.

It's possible that the climate itself will make some of the decisions. Harsh winters left Ontario's vinifera grape growers with much-reduced crops in 2003 and 2005, and some varieties (such as Merlot and Sauvignon Blanc) were particularly hard hit. Some vines were killed outright, and many more were damaged to the point of not producing fruit the following year.

It seems likely that there will be dramatic changes in the composition of Ontario's vineyards, as producers pay more attention to the suitability of vine varieties not to Ontario broadly, but to the specific locations of their vineyards. The division of Niagara Peninsula into sub-appellations (see pages 31–33) was underpinned by the identification of several distinct climatic and soil sub-regions along the Peninsula. Likewise, growers in Ontario's other wine regions have identified marked temperature and soil differences in specific districts.

A third area of change has been greater attention to yields. One of the attractions of labrusca and some hybrid varieties was that they produced vast amounts of fruit. But winemakers now know that controlling yields is essential for making quality wine, and green harvesting (removing some bunches of grapes before they ripen so as to allow the rest to develop more concentrated flavours) is now the rule is Ontario vineyards.

There has also been a shift in winemaking techniques in Ontario. Many wineries, especially newer ones, are stressing the importance of gravity-fed production, which means that wine is moved by gravity, rather than pump, from one stage of the winemaking process to the next. The first Ontario winery to adopt this system systematically was

**AN ARTIFICIAL BIRD
TO DETER THE REAL ONES**

Malivoire, and the newest wineries, like Stratus, Flat Rock, Tawse, and Norman Hardie, have also been designed to employ gravity.

Winemaking and viticultural knowledge, as well as research on the climate and soils on Ontario wine country, have been boosted by two programs in Niagara, one at Brock University and the other at Niagara College. The Cool Climate Oenology and Viticulture Institute (CCOVI) at Brock University launched a B.Sc. in Oenology and Viticulture in 1996, and its graduates are already well represented throughout the region and in wineries elsewhere in Canada and abroad. Meanwhile, Niagara College's Winery and Viticulture Technician program, which opened in 2000, covers not only viticulture and winemaking but also wine marketing, and its graduates are already starting to make their presence felt in the region and elsewhere.

SELLING ONTARIO WINE

Ontario wines are just starting to make an impact in North America and the wider world. Icewine has been the leader here. Ontario icewines regularly freeze out the competition in the icewine and dessert wine categories in international competitions. The most successful market for icewine is Asia, where it has become such a luxury product that it's counterfeited in the same way as Rolex watches and Gucci bags. A wine called "icewine" is made in New Zealand by artificially freezing grapes, but an international agreement signed by Canada, Germany, Austria, and the United States limits the use of the name to wines made from grapes frozen on the vine. The Cool Climate Oenology and Viticulture Institute at Brock University has brought wine merchants and professionals from Asia to train them in the characteristics to look for in genuine icewine.

There is some concern that Ontario might get trapped in an icewine ghetto. Icewine reinforces an image of Canada as a place permanently covered with snow and ice. The only display featuring Canada at Vinopolis, the permanent wine exhibition in London (England), is a blown-up photograph of a picker harvesting grapes for icewine. He's wearing a padded jacket, mittens, and a wool hat, and his beard is frosted with ice from his breath. Crouching before frozen grapes hanging from icy wires, he looks like a figure in the Soviet Gulag, and he contrasts starkly with the common image of pickers smiling as they happily harvest grapes in the sun.

It will take marketing skill to educate foreign wine professionals, not to mention the international wine-buying public, that Ontario isn't permanently under snow and can produce quality table wine. Some Ontario wineries have made export progress in the United States, especially in neighbouring states like New York, and a 2004 agreement with the European Union gave Canadian wine access to Europe. But with a series of reduced harvests through to 2005, Ontario hasn't been able to take full advantage of the export opportunities.

Canadian diplomats are doing their bit to promote sales. In 2004 the federal government created the position of Canadian Wine Promotion Coordinator to facilitate Canada's diplomatic missions abroad when ordering Canadian wines. The aim is to ensure that Canadian wines are served at receptions and official dinners. A successful pilot project that year saw Canadian wine shipped to embassies and high commissions in Asia and Europe,

**MANY ONTARIO WINERIES OFFER
RESTAURANTS AND EVENTS FACILITIES**

OPPOSITE: **HARD WORK: THE HIDDEN SIDE
OF WINEMAKING ROMANTICISM**

and by mid-2005, 44 Ontario wineries (and another 16 from British Columbia) were participating in the program.

The market that remains to be developed is Ontario itself. VQA wines from Ontario account for about 17 percent of wine sales in the province, with non-VQA and foreign-Ontario blends accounting for another 26 percent. Having more than two-fifths of sales doesn't seem bad, but it pales against the share that French, Italian, Australian, and Californian wines have in their domestic markets. The Ontario wine industry's strategic plan aims to expand Ontario's market share to a quite modest 60 percent by 2020.

VQA CERTIFICATION

Since 1999, Vintner's Quality Alliance rules have had the force of law in Ontario. For a wine to carry the VQA decal, it must be made from a minimum percentage of grapes from a Designated Viticultural Area. A wine with a VQA Ontario designation must be wholly made from Ontario grapes. The critical issue here is where the grapes were grown, not where the wine was made. A wine with a regional appellation, like VQA Niagara Peninsula or VQA Lake Erie North Shore, must be made from grapes at least 85 percent of which were grown in the region. The rest of the grapes may have been grown elsewhere in Ontario. If a wine bears the name of one of the sub-appellations in Niagara Peninsula, it must be made exclusively from grapes grown in the sub-appellation.

VQA wines must have a minimum percentage of grapes from the labelled appellation and vintage, and a minimum percentage of the variety stated on the label. VQA rules also specify what winemakers can and can't do. They can chaptalize (add sugar), for example, but they can't stretch wine with water. Finally, before wine is accepted for VQA certification, producers must submit bottles for analysis and also for tasting by a panel of wine professionals, who consider the wine's quality and varietal typicity.

In short, VQA certification offers consumers various guarantees of quality and authenticity. It falls between restrictive wine laws like France's Appellation d'Origine Contrôlée and the United States' American Viticultural Area system, which controls appellations and varietal content, but doesn't require a quality test. Like all wine laws, the VQA has its critics who regard it as either too restrictive or too permissive, and its rules will undoubtedly continue to evolve with changing conditions.

CURRENT ISSUES

Amid the promising signs for Ontario wine, there are a number of contentious issues. One is wines that are sold under "Product of Canada" and "Cellared in Canada" labels. Under provincial law, wineries importing wine in bulk to Ontario must add a por-tion of Ontario wine to it, and "Cellared in Canada" wine must contain at least 30 percent Ontario wine. The Ontario content was reduced to a minimum 10 percent in 2003 because of the short crop following the harsh 2002–03 winter, and then to only one percent in 2005 because of the shortage of Ontario grapes that year.

The issue isn't the blending of wines from different countries, but the labelling. Consumers often buy "Product of Canada" and "Cellared in Canada" wines thinking they're Canadian wines, and their confusion is compounded by the fact that these wines are often shelved in the Ontario section of LCBO stores. Many small producers of exclusively Ontario wine are irritated by these practices, which they believe undermine the integrity of Ontario wine. In 2005, when blended wines could have as much as 99 percent foreign content, the government mandated clearer distinctions in the way the LCBO displayed the predominantly foreign wines.

Other complaints focus on the dominance of the LCBO in Ontario wine retail market. The LCBO isn't a true monopoly, because Ontario consumers can buy wine elsewhere. Some wineries, like Colio Estate and Château des Charmes, operate retail stores, but the biggest chain by far is Vincor's Wine Rack, which has 160 outlets across Ontario, many of them in supermarkets. Wineries also sell wine directly from their own premises, and consumers can order wines for home delivery directly from wineries or from online wine-shipping services.

Even so, the LCBO sells about 85 percent of the wine in the province, and the situation isn't likely to change soon. In 2005, a commission set up by the provincial government to examine the sale of beverage alcohol in Ontario recommended turning over all alcohol retailing to the private sector. The government quickly rejected the recommendation. Although it's possible Ontario might eventually allow private stores not linked to wineries, it's unlikely to happen very soon.

The LCBO General List tends to carry wines from the bigger Ontario producers, like Jackson-Triggs, Inniskillin, Kittling Ridge, Henry of Pelham,

Cave Spring, and Pelee Island. Unlike small producers, they can supply the volumes the LCBO needs for its cross-province operations. The LCBO does purchase from smaller producers for its Vintages stores, and also has a program to stock wine from smaller producers in selected stores. In recent years there have been some changes that loosened the LCBO's grip on retailing. For example, wineries can now supply restaurants and other licensees directly, rather than having to go through the LCBO.

Still, many Ontario wine producers complain about a system they see as limiting their ability to sell their wine. From the vineyard at his Mountain Road Estate Winery, Steve Kocsis can see the skyline of Toronto, but he says, "I might as well be looking at the minarets of Baghdad," because he can't get his wine into the Toronto market.

THE FUTURE

Who would dare predict the future of an industry as young as Ontario's wine industry? There are many signs of prosperity. Four or five new wineries have opened in Niagara each year since 2000, and more are on the drawing boards. Vincor is working on a new venture, Le Clos Jordanne, with the big French company Groupe Boisset. The winery, designed by noted architect Frank Gehry, is slated to open in 2008. Other wineries are planned for the Lake Erie North Shore and Prince Edward County regions.

On the other hand, the climate played havoc with grape harvests throughout Ontario between 2003 and 2005, and forcefully reminded the province's winemakers that their industry is a branch of agriculture. But Ontario is hardly the only wine region in the world to go through ups and downs because of climate. The expectation in Ontario is that, within the climatic and economic cycles that influence harvests, production, and sales, the overall trend will be healthy growth.

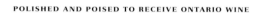

POLISHED AND POISED TO RECEIVE ONTARIO WINE

NIAGARA PENINSULA: CLIMATE, LAND, AND VINES

NOT ONLY VINES PREFER NIAGARA'S WINTERS. PEOPLE OVER THE AGE OF 65 MAKE UP AS HIGH A PROPORTION OF NIAGARA'S POPULATION AS RESIDENTS OF VICTORIA, BRITISH COLUMBIA.

LAKE, BENCH, AND ESCARPMENT

The Niagara Peninsula is far and away the most important of Ontario's wine regions, whether in terms of vineyard area, the number of wineries, or the volume and value of wine produced. It has some 15,000 acres (6,000 hectares) of vines and 60 wineries, ranging from large outfits turning out hundreds of thousands of cases a year to small producers, which sell a few thousand. The Niagara Peninsula is also Canada's most important wine region, producing up to 80 percent of Canada's wine grapes in good years.

As you drive along the Queen Elizabeth Way (known locally as the QEW), which runs east-west through much of the region and links Toronto to the U.S. border at Niagara Falls, you can see what makes the Niagara Peninsula so suitable for viticulture. On one side of the highway lies Lake Ontario, often calm, sometimes with whitecaps. On a clear day, you can't necessarily see forever, but you can see the Toronto skyline: the CN Tower, SkyDome, and the corporate towers.

On the other side of the highway rises the Niagara Escarpment, a treelined ridge that rises to 575 feet (175 metres) above sea level in places. It marks the shore of an older and deeper lake, Lake Iroquois, of which present-day Lake Ontario is what's left. The Escarpment runs from the American side of the Canada-U.S. border, more than 700 kilometres into northern Ontario, then back into the U.S. in Michigan.

OPPOSITE: **GRAPES IN THEIR HARD, TART, YOUTHFUL AGE**

The Escarpment doesn't rise like a perpendicular bluff from a plain. Along the length of the Niagara region, the land slopes gently back from the lakeshore and then rises in a series of "benches," sloping steps that eventually meet the limestone cliffs. Depending on the area, the escarpment then rises

BIRTH OF A BUNCH

100 to 160 feet (30 to 50 metres) above the highest bench. The bench is generically known as the Niagara Bench, and specific sections of it are named after nearby communities, such as Beamsville (the Beamsville Bench) and St. David's (St. David's Bench).

Lake Ontario, the Benches, and the Escarpment create the climatic conditions for viticulture in the Niagara Peninsula. Lake Ontario doesn't freeze over during the winter. During the cold months, its waters give off warm air that's carried across land until it reaches the Escarpment. As these winds hit the Benches and limestone cliffs, they're deflected upward until they meet cold air coming off the top of the Escarpment. The cold air traps the warmer air, which circulates in a convection current and creates a microclimate on the land between escarpment and lake.

What this means for vines is that they're less likely to be subjected to the extreme cold that kills or damages them. Winter temperatures always drop well below freezing (if they didn't, Niagara Peninsula couldn't produce icewine), but they're moderate compared to those of the surrounding area. Not only vines prefer Niagara's winters. People over the age of 65 make up as high a proportion of Niagara's population as residents of Victoria, British Columbia, which for many years was the retirement capital of Canada. More and more Ontarians seeking milder winters, once their working years are over, have settled in the Niagara region.

If the lake acts as a warming influence during the winter, it does the opposite in spring, when lake breezes cool the land between the shore and the Escarpment. The cooler air prevents the vines from maturing too early, when they'd be vulnerable to late frosts. Then, during the growing season from June to September breezes from the lake hit the escarpment and bounce back toward the lake. Escarpment and lake combine to provide constant air movement across the region, ensuring that vines and grapes dry quickly after spring and summer rain, reducing the risks of disease, and also reducing the size of grapes, giving them more concentrated flavours. As the grapes reach optimum ripeness in September and October, the residual warm breezes off Lake Ontario prevent the land from cooling too quickly. This can lengthen the growing season and leads to many Indian summers, periods of very warm weather during the fall.

There are differences in climate, sometimes significant and sometimes subtle, among Niagara's regions. For example, the Benches, which are higher and farther from the influence of the lake, tend to be cooler than much of the lower-lying flat land of Niagara-on-the-Lake during the growing season. Winemaker Darryl Brooker, who lives in Beamsville and drives to work at Hillebrand Estates in Niagara-on-the-Lake, says that he often sees temperatures rise "two, three, sometimes five degrees" during the short trip. The north-facing slopes along the Bench moderate extremes of summer heat and give more cool-climate varietal typicity in aromatic whites and in heat-averse reds like Pinot Noir.

Variations also occur in the kind of soil found in the Niagara region. Overall the soil is a complex mix of glacial deposits, with the main difference between the lakeshore areas, where sandy loam predominates, and the Bench areas, where soil has more clay content and is heavier. The Bench soil drains well but retains enough moisture to benefit vines during the dry period of the growing season.

Finally, topographical characteristics like slope, sun exposure, and proximity to water, all have an impact on the ways vines grow and grapes ripen. Some districts are less prone to frost than others during the shoulder seasons; some are consistently warmer than others throughout the year, while others are more exposed to wind.

APPELLATIONS AND SUB-APPELLATIONS

With some 15,000 acres (6,000 hectares) of vines (about the same as Australia's Barossa Valley), Niagara Peninsula is a mid-sized appellation (designated wine region) in global terms. It's much larger than appellations like Romanée-Conti in Burgundy, which comprises only 63 acres (25 hectares), but it pales against Bordeaux, which measures in at 300,000 planted acres (120,000 hectares).

Yet as modest as it is in size, Niagara Peninsula encompasses many variations in climate, soil structure, and topography, all of which affect grapes and wine styles, and many wine producers wanted to signal the distinctiveness of their vineyards on their labels. The most prominent have been the wineries located on the Beamsville Bench and wineries sourcing grapes from vineyards located there. Several wineries, like Thirty Bench and Crown Bench, incorporated their location into their corporate names. Others show Bench vineyard locations

THE VARIED LANDSCAPE OF ONTARIO WINE COUNTRY

A NEW VINEYARD ON THE LAKESHORE

on labels, like the Château des Charmes, St. David's Bench-designated wines.

To make the use of these terms more systematic and consistent, the Niagara Peninsula was divided into a number of sub-appellations. It was a drawn-out and often contentious process. Some wineries favoured the sub-appellations because they'd enable them to indicate their vineyards more precisely. Just as Volnay is more prestigious than the generic Burgundy appellation and Alexander Valley more than Sonoma Valley within which it's located, so a smaller sub-appellation might carry more cachet than Niagara Peninsula. Beyond commercial considerations, some winemakers argued that sub-appellations more accurately reflected the micro-climates and geological profile (often referred to as the terroir) of their vineyards more sensitively.

Arguments against the sub-appellations included fears that multiple appellations would confuse consumers. Some cited the example of Burgundy, a small region with a hundred appellations in several tiers—and one that drives all but the most knowledgeable wine lovers to distraction, if not to drink. Others argued that it was simply too early to designate sub-appellations, and that more time was needed before climatic and soil variations and their effects on grapes were properly understood. Even when the principle of sub-appellations was accepted, debates continued over the number of sub-appellations, their boundaries, and their names.

The final sub-appellation system became law in 2005. There are 10 sub-appellations, each covering a defined geographical area. Four are named as benches (Beamsville Bench, Twenty Mile Bench, Short Hills Bench, and St. David's Bench), three for the lakeshore (Lincoln Lakeshore, Creek Shores, and Niagara Lakeshore), and three for other geographical features: Niagara River, Four Mile Creek, and Vinemount Ridge. There are also two collective sub-appellations: Niagara Escarpment comprises the three Bench sub-appellations west of St. Catharines (Beamsville Bench, Twenty Mile Bench, and Short Hills Bench), while Niagara-on-the-Lake comprises all four appellations east of St. Catharines (Niagara Lakeshore, Four Mile Creek, St. David's Bench, and Niagara River).

Wineries can choose to label their wine as "Niagara Peninsula," as one of the sub-appellations alone, or as "Niagara Peninsula" plus a sub-appellation. If wineries choose to use one of the sub-appellations, 100 percent of the grapes in the wine must be sourced from it.

THE GRAPES

Most of the wine grapes now grown in the Niagara Peninsula belong to the Vitis vinifera species. It includes varieties that are often referred to as "classic," "noble," or "international," such as Chardonnay, Merlot, Riesling, Cabernet Sauvignon, and Pinot Noir. But there are still extensive plantings of hybrid varieties, especially Baco Noir and Vidal. Baco Noir is a hybrid of an unidentified native North American variety and Folle Blanche, which used to be grown in regions on France's Atlantic coast. One of its strengths is winter-hardiness, which enables it to grow in areas more prone to frosts. It's also one of the earliest-ripening red varieties, which allows for consistent ripening even in years with short growing seasons.

The other widely planted hybrid, Vidal, is the progeny of Ugni Blanc and a Seibel variety, itself a hybrid. In Niagara, Vidal withstands cold weather well and is used mainly to make large volumes of ordinary white wine that's sold as house wine in restaurants throughout the province. Some Niagara producers make higher-quality table wines from Vidal, and it has found a particular niche as one of the varieties most often used for icewine. Like Riesling, Vidal grapes cling tenaciously to the vines during the autumn and winter and, even though many people prefer the acidity and flavours of Riesling ice wine, some of Niagara's foremost ice-wine winemakers prefer Vidal.

Baco Noir and Vidal apart, hybrid grape varieties are disappearing from the Niagara Peninsula. A number of wineries produce Maréchal Foch, which has a following, but many other hybrids that used to be popular have gone. Until the late 1990s, the Thomas & Vaughan winery made small batches of dessert wine from a parcel of Catawba grapes, but they eventually ripped the vines out and replanted with vinifera varieties.

With the exception of Baco Noir and Maréchal Foch and icewine made from Vidal, the Niagara Peninsula's premium wines are made from vinifera grapes. Since the 1980s, growers have tried to identify the right varieties for the region, and now some varieties are recognized as making superior wine from Niagara vineyards. The white varieties that consistently make quality wine are Riesling, Chardonnay, and Sauvignon Blanc. The reds are Cabernet Franc, Gamay, and Pinot Noir, and some wineries have made promising Syrah from young vines. This isn't to overlook excellent wines made from varieties like Gewürztraminer, Viognier, and Chenin Blanc. And although many wineries produce fine wines from Merlot and Cabernet Sauvignon in good vintages, they often have difficulty bringing them to full ripeness. In off-years, they can have off-putting green flavours, and there's some debate about their suitability to the region unless the vines' yields are rigorously controlled.

Even more warmly debated are Pinot Noir and Syrah. Some winemakers are convinced that Niagara won't produce good Pinot Noir, while others, like Lailey Vineyards' Derek Barnett, believe Pinot Noir is the grape variety for their winery. Despite its occasional detractors, Pinot Noir is establishing a reputation in the region. The same debate surrounds Syrah, which some wineries (like Peninsula Ridge) are devoting large areas to, while others shy away from it entirely. But many wineries are moving ahead cautiously with these varieties. The proof of Syrah will come when the vines are mature; most were planted after 2000.

Some recent vintages have sharpened the discussion about the grape varieties that are suitable for the Niagara Peninsula. The winters of 2002–03 and 2004–05 were unusually harsh, with temperatures dropping to –2°F (–19°C) on some parts of the lakeshore and six degrees colder in some inland areas. The cold affected many vines, which reduced crops in the following growing seasons. Some vines were killed outright. Overall, the crop from the 2003 vintage was between 40 and 50 percent lower than the 2002 vintage, which was excellent in quantity and quality, and the 2005 crop was less than half the size of 2004's.

Patterns of these two winters' damage and kill varied from district to district and vineyard to vineyard, depending on exposure and topography. Lower-lying vineyards suffered more, and some varieties proved much more vulnerable than others. Merlot and Sauvignon Blanc were hit especially hard, and in some areas, the 2003 crop of these varieties was down 75 percent from the previous year. Sauvignon Blanc presents a particular problem for the region: it's a grape that makes excellent wines but is vulnerable in colder winters.

The experience of recent winters might well have a long-term impact on the grape varieties cultivated in Niagara. Some growers have decided not to replant Merlot and to focus on varieties that have proved winter-hardy. Wind machines, which disperse cold air, are appearing in more and more vineyards. Some small growers even talk about burying vines to protect them from cold (as is done in Prince Edward County), but this is a difficult and expensive alternative for large vineyards. It's also clear that grape growers have to give even more thought to the places where they plant specific varieties. It makes more sense to plant hardier varieties, like Chardonnay and Riesling, in vineyard sites where there is greater risk of cold air settling.

Short crops from Niagara vineyards in 2003 and 2005 had an enormous impact on the profitability of wineries, and on the availability of Ontario wines to the province's consumers. Still, many winery owners and winemakers shrug when they think about the series of abnormally cold winters. They know

SHOVELLING OUT THE SKINS, SEEDS, AND STEMS
OPPOSITE: **THE FLAT VINESCAPE OF NIAGARA-ON-THE-LAKE**

that viticulture is farming, and that they have to live with the weather. It goes in cycles, they say. With the exception of 2000, the years 1998 to 2002 were very good to excellent, and a few poor vintages in the following years were to be expected.

THE LADYBUG VINTAGE

Climate was only one challenge of Niagara wine in the first years of the new millennium. Another was harmonia axyridis, an orange-yellow variety of the more familiar red and black ladybug. Often called "Asian ladybugs," they were introduced to deal with pests in Niagara's soybean gardens and greenhouses but, in 2001, millions of them migrated to nearby vineyards, especially on the Bench areas. It had been a warm spring and a good long summer, and prospects for a great vintage were justified. In fact, 2001 did turn out to be an exceptional year for wine in Niagara, but much of the vintage was spoiled by what became known simply as "ladybug taint."

The problem with the bugs wasn't that they damaged the leaves or grapes but that when they were disturbed they gave off a liquid that stuck to the grapes. Harvesting really alarmed the bugs, and the result was that, unknown to winemakers, tonnes of grapes processed for the 2001 vintage were contaminated by their residue. What the bugs gave off was pyrazine, a compound that occurs naturally in some grapes. It contributes to the pungency of Sauvignon Blanc and to the flavours of vegetables like bell pepper and asparagus. By itself, pyrazine smells and tastes like bitter peanuts or peanut shell, and these flavours ruined many wines. The off-flavours were discernible in young wines, but they got stronger as the affected wines aged, so what might have been overlooked in a newly-made or just-bottled wine might make it undrinkable a year or two later.

Once the ladybug problem was discovered, wineries took a variety of steps to deal with it. Some destroyed all their affected wine, rather than compromise their reputation. Others tested batches of wines with a view to saving what they could. Most erred on the side of caution, but a few didn't and a number of ladybug-tainted wines went on sale. Some of the affected wines bore the VQA decal, which meant that the VQA's tasters had passed the wines as clean. Again, it's possible that the ladybug flavours became more evident after the wines had been evaluated by the VQA, or that the batches tasted and tested by the VQA weren't affected.

GRAPES EARLY IN THE GROWING SEASON

Unfortunately, once the ladybug problem became known, many consumers refused to buy any 2001 Niagara wines. It was a great shame, because 2001 was an excellent year, and you can find stellar whites and reds from the vintage. And if you want to experience a ladybug-tainted wine, you can do so at Mountain Road Wine Company, where owner Steve Kocsis bottled some affected Riesling and decorated the label with a ladybug. Some visitors who taste it are repelled, he says, but others love it. The back label on the bottles suggests pairing it with a peanut butter and jelly sandwich.

INTO THE DE-STEMMER/CRUSHER

FOLLOWING PAGE: **ICEWINE GRAPES NETTED AGAINST BIRDS**

NIAGARA: GRIMSBY AND BEAMSVILLE

"PART OF THE TERROIR IS THE POOR GUY WHO SITS ON THE TRACTOR ALL DAY."

—STEVE KOCSIS
MOUNTAIN ROAD WINE COMPANY

Grimsby and Beamsville, at the western end of the Niagara Peninsula wine region, have the first major concentration of wineries you come to as you drive down the Queen Elizabeth Way from Toronto. There are only two wineries in Grimsby, but Beamsville has 16, a third of all the wineries in the Peninsula. Most are located on the Beamsville Bench, a series of broad terraces beneath the Niagara escarpment. You can see the topography of this part of Niagara clearly when you drive along King Street, which winds in a series of soft curves along the base of the Bench. On one side, the land slopes gently toward Lake Ontario, while on the other, it rises up sharply toward the Bench. Turn up many of the roads on this side—Mountainview Road, Mountain Road, Cherry Avenue, and their like—and you'll find clusters of wineries.

The label on bottles of Mountain Road Wine Company wines carries a stylized representation of the Beamsville Bench. Toronto's landmark CN Tower and SkyDome sit on one side of the blue lake. On the other side, the land first rises gently from the blue water before raking more dramatically to a sloping plateau—the Bench, shown in vineyard green—which in turn gives way to the higher elevation of the Escarpment. The Bench isn't a continuous, even terrace. It's a complex system of small north-facing slopes, divided by ravines, with varying gradients. The slopes provide good drainage

OPPOSITE: **PREPARING THE
BIRD NETTING**

for the vines, and also drain off cold air, reducing risks of frost.

The Niagara Escarpment protects the Bench from strong south-westerly winds in the spring, and allows it to warm gradually from the month of May onwards. Meanwhile, the breeze from Lake Ontario moderates day and night temperatures during the growing season (which lasts until late October), and the warming influence of the lake ensures that the Bench cools slowly during September and October.

Several wineries signal their location on the Beamsville Bench. Some, like Crown Bench Estates and Thirty Bench Vineyard, have incorporated "Bench" into their names. Others use the word on labels. Beamsville wineries have some of the most attractive settings in the Niagara Peninsula. Many of the Niagara's vineyards, especially those farther east, in Niagara-on-the-Lake, are located on fairly flat sites, and visitors from British Columbia's Okanagan Valley have been known to ask where the mountain and lake views are. There are no mountains in Niagara, but many of the wineries on the Beamsville Bench have good views over Lake Ontario, with Toronto floating on its horizon.

THE WINERIES OF GRIMSBY

Puddicombe Estate Farms and Winery

This most westerly winery on the Niagara Peninsula lies in rolling farmland. Located near the town of Grimsby (named by settlers after the city in northern England) it sits off Regional Road 81, near Fifty Road. That tells you how far west this is because, along the Peninsula, numbers like "Fifty" (as in Fifty Road and Twenty Creek) indicate distance in miles from Niagara Falls. From the road, Puddicombe Estate Farms looks like a combination of theme park, winery, and railway station. In the summer season you can buy fresh produce from the farm, as well as grape and fruit wines. Of the 360 acres (145 hectares) it occupies, 160 (64 hectares) are under vines and 200 (80 hectares) under crops as varied as peaches, apples, pears, cherries, strawberries, and blueberries.

The property has been farmed by the Puddicombe family since 1797. Originally a cattle ranch, it became a tender fruit farm in the early 1900s, and grapes were first planted in the 1940s. The first vinifera varieties, Chardonnay and Gamay, put down roots in 1962, well before vinifera took off more generally in Ontario. More vinifera varieties were added in 1968, and in 1975 Riesling, Pinot Noir, and Colombard joined the list. All the grapes were sold to wineries. In 1989, Murray Puddicombe went into partnership with winemaker Jim Warren, and they set up the Stoney Ridge winery on the Puddicombe Farm site. By 1997 they were producing 27,000 cases of wine, but the partnership ended that year, partly because the business had grown beyond the scale Murray Puddicombe had envisaged. Jim Warren re-established Stoney Ridge farther east, in Vineland, and Puddicombe renamed his winery Puddicombe Estate Farms. Its first vintage was 1998 and the winery opened two years later.

The winemaker today is Murray Puddicombe's daughter, Lindsay, who studied agriculture business at the University of Guelph and was in the first graduating class of the viticulture and oenology program at Niagara College. She made her first vintage in 1999 with Sue-Ann Staff (winemaker at Pillitteri Estates) as consultant.

Lindsay Puddicombe is complimentary about her father. Not only does she praise his skills as a grape grower but, she says, "he has an amazing palate. He picks out all the aromatics." Murray Puddicombe's influence isn't only in the wine, but also in the winery environment. He's a train enthusiast, and there are pictures of trains on the walls of the tasting room ("and everywhere in the house," Lindsay says). There's also rolling stock in the vineyards. A Pullman coach is visible from the tasting bar, and somewhere outside are three tankers and a caboose.

Puddicombe Estate is located beneath the escarpment at the point where it's close to the lake. Despite the good air currents, it gets one or two degrees colder in winter than in many other vineyard sites. Puddicombe grows a good range of varieties that do well in cooler climates, but Merlot,

Cabernet Sauvignon, and Gewürztraminer don't ripen successfully here, so they buy these varieties from growers in warmer parts of the Peninsula.

Lindsay Puddicombe aims to make aromatic whites and fruit-forward reds. They include some intensely fruit-driven Chardonnays, a quite delicate Riesling, and Cabernet Franc reserves that show very good typicity. Puddicombe is also the only Niagara winery to grow and vinify Colombard, which makes a crisp white with good fruit character. The train theme comes through in a New York Muscat called "Grand Central" and a couple of blends: Station White (Seyval, Vidal, and Riesling) and Station Red (Gamay, Cabernet Franc, and, intriguingly, a little Cabernet Franc Icewine).

Kittling Ridge Estate Wines and Spirits

Grimsby's other winery, Kittling Ridge, which sits on a service road alongside the Queen Elizabeth Way, is one of Ontario's mid-sized wineries and one of only two privately owned distilleries left in the province. It's also one of the few wineries to have no vineyards of its own. Instead, Kittling Ridge partners with 25 grape growers, two-thirds from the Bench and a third from Niagara-on-the-Lake, to meet the needs of its 150,000 cases of wine a year.

Owner John Hall started out in the early 1970s as a winemaker, and in 1992 set out to open his own winery. He found a small distillery in Grimsby that was making great eau-de-vie, he says, but this wasn't Europe, and there was really no market for it. "But then I looked at the distillery and said to myself, 'My goodness, if this was a winery, it would be one of the best in the region.'" Hall bought the distillery when its owner retired in 1992 and developed a winery, which he called Kittling Ridge.

Why "Kittling Ridge"? John Hall says that one fine day in March 1993, just after he had bought the distillery and was trying to think of a name for his winery, he drove to the top of the Niagara Escarpment to have lunch. He pulled into a conservation park and was eating his sandwich when he saw a group of people watching the sky with binoculars. It turned out they were birdwatchers, following some of the 10,000 to 20,000 hawks, eagles, and

other birds of prey that migrate north each spring through the Niagara area.

When they get over the Escarpment, the birds ride the updrafts of warm air, called thermals, which are created when warm spring winds blow off Lake Ontario against the limestone cliffs and are

GAZEBO, GRAPES, AND WATER

deflected upwards. Birdwatchers refer to the birds' floating on thermals as "kittling," and the name Kittling Ridge came out of that, Hall says. "The same reasons these birds come here year after year—the warm air from the lake and the protection of the Escarpment—create a microclimate that is conducive to grape growing."

Hall's aim is to provide superior wine at an affordable price. "While it's not too difficult to make the finest-tasting wine in the world, the challenge is to make very good-tasting wine at a reasonable price." The Kittling Ridge range covers many varieties and styles, including late-harvest wines and icewine. The first icewine (1992) won the Grand Gold at Vinitaly. There's a premium VQA Niagara Peninsula line called Symmetry that includes Chardonnays (aged in French and American oak),

Riesling, Gewürztraminer, Cabernet Sauvignon, and Old Vines Foch. Between 200 and 400 cases of each Symmetry varietal are made each year, and the line is sold only at the winery stores. In 1996, Kittling Ridge purchased the small Cullotta winery, which owned six retail stores (four in Toronto, one in Barrie, and one in London) that provided it with invaluable outlets for its wines and spirits.

Then there's the distillery, which gave Hall a whole new dimension to work in. He began to think of the way winemaking and distilling relate to each other and quickly learned that distillers need a lot more patience. "With winemaking, you can have a wine out in a year or two, but with whisky, you have to wait six, eight, ten years." He started distilling and brought his winemaking knowledge and skills to it. "I treat each grain—rye, barley, corn—as you

would a varietal grape, bringing out the specific taste characteristics of each varietal grain." Kittling Ridge's production of 400,000 cases of spirits a year is mostly made up of vodka, whisky, rum, and brandy.

Its signature product, Icewine & Brandy, is a blend of Vidal icewine and seven-year-old brandy. Hall says it has wonderful flavours: "It cuts the sweetness of the icewine in half and brings vanilla and chocolate flavours out in the brandy." It was released in 1993 and has won more than 25 international tasting awards. "It brings together in one bottle," Hall says, "the winemaker's art and the stillmaster's craft."

THE WINERIES OF BEAMSVILLE
Peninsula Ridge Estates Winery
The most westerly winery seated on the Beamsville Bench is Peninsula Ridge Estates. It has a historical connection to Beamsville in that it's located on

THE NET BENEFIT: PROTECTION AGAINST BIRDS

property first settled by William Kitchen, a business partner of Jacob Beam, who gave his name to the town. Kitchen, who was married to Alice Beam, was a loyalist who came to Niagara from New Jersey in 1790 and received a British land grant to settle the area. Kitchen and Beam built a gristmill, and Peninsula Ridge's winery facilities are located where the mill once stood.

The mill might be gone, but other historic buildings remain and have been integrated into the winery. The retail shop is a reconstructed post-and-beam barn from 1885. The winery's highly rated restaurant is located in a Queen Anne revival house built the same year for William Dennis Kitchen, the original settler's grandson, who farmed soft fruit in the area. There was also a carriage house on the site, but it couldn't be salvaged. A new carriage house, now used for events like weddings and receptions, was built on the footprint of the original.

The pedigree of Peninsula Ridge's land might go back centuries, but the winery itself was established only recently by Norman Beal. Its first vintage was 2000, but Peninsula Ridge has established its reputation so quickly that it's hard to believe it's so new. The winery has matured so rapidly that in 2004 the winemaker, Jean-Pierre Colas, started doing verticals of some of his wines to examine their evolution.

Peninsula Ridge may be the creation of Norman Beal, who was born in Niagara, but his first career was in the energy business in western Canada and the United States. Beal's work took him around the world, and these travels gave him the chance to pursue his passion for wine. By the mid-1990s, he figured it was time for a career change, and started looking at locations for a winery in California and Long Island. But Beal's sister, who was involved in viticulture in Niagara, persuaded him to look at opportunities here. Beal says he was pretty skeptical at first, remembering Niagara wines of the 1970s made with labrusca grapes and sparkling wines made with added sugar. But he came to Niagara in 1998 to have a look and visited established wineries like Cave Spring Cellars. He was impressed by what he tasted, especially the whites, and amazed

UNPICKED GRAPES FROM FALL HARVEST

that a wine region could make such a dramatic turnaround in such a short time.

Beal decided to open a winery and settled on the Beamsville Bench property because of its soil, the climate, and also because of the views and the historic buildings. "So much about wine is old, it's hard to give a new winery a sense of history," he says. "But in these buildings, we had it."

Wine professionals often say that wine is 80 (or 70, or 90) percent made in the vineyards, and no one would argue that great wine can be made only from first-class fruit—which comes from the right vines grown in the right conditions. But neither would anyone dispute that you need a first-class winemaker to produce the wine. Norman Beal found his winemaker on a visit to France in 1999, when he met Jean-Pierre Colas, head winemaker at prestigious Domaine Laroche in Chablis. Colas had made wine there through the 1990s and had distinguished himself by having one of his 1996 wines declared "white wine of the year" by *Wine Spectator*. He'd also made wine in Chile.

Colas visited Niagara a month after he and Beal met, and together they embarked on a gruelling one-week tour of Niagara vineyards and wineries

STAINLESS STEEL, THE PARTNER TO OAK IN WINEMAKING

OPPOSITE: **GRAPES GAIN SUGAR INTENSITY AS THEY SHRIVEL**

so that Colas could make his own assessment of the region's potential. "Jean-Pierre seemed to enjoy it," Beal recalls, "but I was pretty wined-out after four days!" Colas liked what he saw and tasted and came to Peninsula Ridge in 2000 for the winery's first full vintage. (In 1999, several winemakers—including Colas in France, via cell phone and fax—had made a small amount of wine.) He landed in Toronto just two days before starting his first crush at Peninsula Ridge.

Although Jean-Pierre Colas came from Chablis, where he made only white wines, slightly more than half his production at Peninsula Ridge is red, mainly Cabernet Sauvignon, Merlot, and Cabernet Franc, but increasingly Syrah. Unlike some Niagara winemakers, he's not enthusiastic about the prospects for Pinot Noir.

Both Beal and Colas are bullish about Syrah, though, and in Beal's words, "we're sticking our necks out on this one." It's not that Peninsula Ridge is the only Niagara winery producing Syrah, but they have the largest planting in the region and Beal expects it will soon be the second most important varietal (after Sauvignon Blanc) in Peninsula Ridge's portfolio. Colas aims to make his Syrah in a Northern Rhône style—complex, well structured, with marked pepper notes. Peninsula Ridge's Syrah vines are young—they were planted in 2001—and the wines will develop more structure as the vines age. Colas warns that you shouldn't expect it to taste like a Shiraz in the Australian style: "If you like fat, jammy, and sweet, you're out of luck." Syrah is also included (along with Cabernet Sauvignon, Cabernet Franc, and Merlot, all Bordeaux varieties) in a blend called Arcanum, a stylish red that Jean-Pierre Colas calls "a bridge" between Bordeaux and the Rhône.

If Norman Beal has one reservation about his reds, it's that they're drunk too young. He'd like to hold some back and sell them when they have some bottle-age, and recommends holding his reds for a few years. Older vintages, which in Peninsula Ridge terms means as far back as 2000, are available on the winery's restaurant wine list.

As much as Jean-Pierre Colas has rallied to reds at Peninsula Ridge, he's still passionate about his whites. His 2000 Sauvignon Blanc helped put the variety on the Niagara Peninsula map. It had full-on pungent fruit with stylish, racy acidity, and once the word got out, the wine sold through quickly. It helped to establish the winery's reputation early on, and each year's Sauvignon Blanc sells out within three months of going on sale. The winery grows and contracts more Sauvignon Blanc than any other in the Niagara region, and it's increasing production to the point that it will represent its largest variety.

It's only a matter of time before Niagara Peninsula Sauvignon Blancs, like Peninsula Ridge's, gain much wider recognition, because they challenge some of the best from New Zealand and France for quality. Although Jean-Pierre Colas is from France,

JORDAN HARBOUR

and spent two months in New Zealand looking at growing and winemaking techniques, his aim is to make Sauvignon Blanc in a style that's distinct from both New Zealand and France.

As you'd expect of a Chablis winemaker, Colas has a special affection for Chardonnay. He makes it in several styles, some aged in oak and others in stainless steel to produce the lean, mineral style associated with Chablis. The premium Peninsula Ridge Chardonnay is named INOX for the stainless steel it's fermented and aged in. It's a classic, lean Chardonnay, the kind the ABC (Anything But Chardonnay) crowd overlook at their risk.

The icon Peninsula Ridge white, though, is Equinox, a blend of Chardonnay, Sauvignon Blanc, and Viognier, which are the winery's best white varieties. Norman Beal says they debated for some time whether the market was ready for a premium white blend; he remembered a host of white-blend jug wines from the 1970s. But Equinox has been very successful, further evidence of Niagara's vinous maturity.

Peninsula Ridge has innovated in a number of ways. Jean-Pierre Colas was scarcely off the plane when he made his first icewine in 2000, and he made a second vintage in 2001, but none since. He says, provocatively, that it's easy enough to make, but he's not interested. Yes, there's an export market, but domestic sales are sluggish and hardly anyone who comes to Peninsula Ridge's tasting bar asks for it. Norman Beal likes the icewine his winery made in 2000 and 2001, but sighs, "It's hard to get a French winemaker to make icewine." That's not to say that Colas lacks a spirit of innovation. One of his products is Ratafia, a blend of plum juice and grape alcohol. It's fairly high in alcohol (18 percent) and made in the style of French Mistelle.

Daniel Lenko Estate Winery

Along King Street from Peninsula Ridge is Daniel Lenko Estate Winery, named for the member of the Lenko family who founded the winery. Daniel's grandparents, John and Agnes, had left the appalling conditions in Ukraine in the 1930s and settled in Manitoba. They bought the 30-acre (12-hectare) property in Beamsville in 1947 and grew fruit and grapes. The grapes were mostly Concord, and were sold to various wineries for decades.

In 1959, well before vinifera fever hit Niagara, their son, Bill, ripped out some of the Concord and planted Chardonnay. This was one of the first plantings of that variety in the region (Brights Wines had released a Chardonnay in 1956) and Bill Lenko's Chardonnay vineyard soon took on star status. Over the years, it produced a number of award-winning wines made by different wineries. Today, Daniel Lenko makes stunning Chardonnays from these old vines.

In the 1970s, as vinifera plantings spread through Niagara, Bill Lenko replaced all his remaining Concord vines, starting with varieties like Merlot (his were among the earliest plantings in Ontario) and Cabernet Sauvignon. They collected awards for various wineries, and Bill Lenko's achievements led him to being crowned Ontario's "Grape King" in 1990. It was only a matter of time before the Lenko name made the leap from vineyard to label, and Bill Lenko's son, Daniel, then in his early 30s, carried the project forward. He says he wishes he had done it earlier, "but my dad was still farming and there's a delicate balance between father and son." Lenko engaged Niagara's iconic winemaker, Jim Warren, to make wine under the Daniel Lenko name from the 1999 harvest, and in 2000 he opened the winery.

No wine venture could have had a better start: the 1999 Daniel Lenko Chardonnay won "Best Chardonnay in Ontario," and it was followed by Best Merlot in 2002, Best Pinot Noir in 2004, and many other awards. Daniel Lenko himself was named "Grape King" for 2002–03 by the Grape Growers of Ontario, making him and his father the second father-son pair to win the title.

Daniel Lenko Estate was soon recognized as producing some of the region's best wines, to the point of reaching a sort of cult status. It seemed that people would pay well to get hold of the highest-demand wines, and Lenko devised a selling strategy that can only be described as different. While some wineries have stimulated demand for certain wines by limiting customers to one or two bottles, Lenko started to require his clients to buy some of his wines in 12-bottle case lots. He tried it first with his 2002 Old Vines Merlot, and when that wine sold well, he added the 2003 Reserve Riesling to the by-the-case-only program.

Lenko aims to sell his 5,000-case production as quickly as possible each year—ideally by mid-summer—and then to close during the busy tourist season in Ontario wine country. It's not that he's shy—on the contrary, he's gregarious, confident, and outgoing and seems to enjoy the limelight that shines on a successful young winery owner—but he wants to spend the late summer and fall in the vineyards. So he puts up a Tasting Room Closed for the Season sign, which must puzzle tourists.

Another reason for the strategy is that the winery has no real tasting room. If you do want to taste and buy Daniel Lenko wines, you have to knock on the door of the brick farmhouse where Daniel's parents, Bill and Helen, still live. More than one first-time visitor has hesitated and looked around for a "real" tasting room, before knocking. If you miss the big sign at the entrance to the driveway, a small sign on the railing by the door of the house will read either Open or Closed.

Assuming you visit during the "Open" season, between February and mid-summer, the tasting is done in the kitchen—often while the legendary Helen Lenko rolls pastry and fills her legendary pies and makes her legendary cakes and cookies. Occasionally, she comes out from behind her flour-dusted counter, wipes her hands on her apron, and takes out the photograph album. It's full of pictures of dignitaries sitting at the kitchen table, tasting

WINTER PRUNING

wine. There's a nice shot of John Ralston Saul, husband of former Governor General Adrienne Clarkson and a great supporter of Canadian wine, with a clutch of ambassadors he'd brought to the winery for a tasting.

Their various excellencies smile from the photograph in the album, and while they might just be wearing their protocol faces, they're as likely to have been very pleased at what they were tasting, for Daniel Lenko wines live up to their reputation. The varietals, white and red, are notable for their intense fruit flavours, their complexity, and their elegant texture.

It's not that Daniel Lenko hasn't thought of building a winery with a dedicated tasting bar. There are architect's drawings for a substantial and elegant structure, but they're tucked away for now. There's a kind of cachet in being able to chat to Bill Lenko as he drops into the kitchen and in picking up a few

pointers from Helen Lenko on how to stop your pastry sticking to the rolling pin. Good old country hospitality works as well as sophisticated concierges ushering visitors into cool, sleek tasting rooms and retail shops. It's just a different approach. Daniel Lenko signals this with a roadside sign that replaces the Closed for the Season notice in February: Vines by Dad. Pies by Mum. Wines by Son.

There was a shift in style when Jim Warren ceased making wines at Daniel Lenko in 2002. His place was taken by Ilya Senchuk who, like the Lenkos, is from Manitoba, and who is one of the many graduates of Brock University's Cool Climate Oenology and Viticulture Institute who are now working in the region. Senchuk and Lenko are now making the wines, especially the reds (Merlot, Cabernet Franc, Cabernet Sauvignon, Pinot Noir, and Meritage) with longer skin contact so as to give them more structure and aging potential. It's a sign of a maturing winery and maturing wine consumers, and besides, if you're going to buy wine by the case, you want to be able to cellar some of it for a few years.

Angels Gate Winery

Along King Street and up Mountainview Road, a little off the beaten track (which makes it so important to explore Niagara's well-signposted byways) is Angels Gate Winery. The name derives from the property, which was once owned by the Congregation of Missionary Sisters of Christian Charity. It was also a mink farm in the 1950s and 1960s, and lay abandoned for decades when the mink market declined, but it was eventually planted in grapes in 1995. The first vintage from the property was 2000, when three wines were made: a Chardonnay, an Old Vines Chardonnay, and a Zweigelt. The Zweigelt was labelled "Red 2000," because the producers felt people were having a difficult time pronouncing the name of the grape.

Construction of the winery building began in 2001, and the owners—a consortium of mainly business people from Toronto—decided to evoke the nuns rather than the minks. Angels Gate (no apostrophe) opened the following year, and the building now houses not only the winery but a retail store, tasting room, and rooms for functions. In summer, the deck becomes a small restaurant, where diners can look out over vines to the lake.

Angels Gate has a total of 56 acres (22 hectares) of vines in three vineyards. The 10-acre (4-hectare) estate vineyard has Chardonnay, Gewürztraminer, Cabernet Franc, and Cabernet Sauvignon. The other vineyards, one in Beamsville and the other at the end of Mountainview Road, are planted in three white varieties (Chardonnay, Riesling, and Sauvignon Blanc) and five reds (Cabernet Franc and Sauvignon, Merlot, Pinot Noir, and Syrah). Together, the vineyards contribute about a third of the winery's needs, and the rest is bought from other growers on long-term contracts.

Although membership of the owning consortium has changed during Angels Gate's short life, its winemaker, Natalie Spytkowsky, has been there since the first vintage was completely done on site, in 2001. Spytkowsky is a winemaker who grew up with vineyard dirt under her nails. A native of Niagara, she first worked at pruning and tying vines, but gravitated toward winemaking. She was an assistant winemaker at two Niagara wineries, Strewn and Creekside, and also worked at Creekside's sister winery in Nova Scotia, Blomidon Ridge (which was then known as Habitant Vineyards). In 1999, Spytkowsky started her own business, a laboratory providing analytical services to wineries. It attracted clients from 40 wineries in Canada and the United States, but it was so time-consuming that she abandoned it in 2003 to focus on making wine for Angels Gate.

Spytkowsky sums up her winemaking philosophy as "less is more," by which she means that "less fining, less filtering, less moving, less racking"

MIDSUMMER RIPENING

enables her "to capture more of the aromatics, the essences, and the structure in the bottle." She wants to educate wine lovers that "a little bit of sediment in the bottle is okay, and that there are reasons for it, and that it's not an imperfection." She finds that customers are ready to understand that wine, especially red, needn't be crystal clear. They understand,

A YOUNG VINE DEVELOPS

OPPOSITE: **SPRING IN THE VINEYARD**

she says, that this is what Angels Gate is moving towards: "fuller-bodied wines, higher-end wines, without stripping everything out of it." Spytkowsky points out that there are no second labels at Angels Gate, "no inferior wines: everything is high-end." But she hastens to add that this refers to quality, not price, and that she gives the same attention to the inexpensive Vidal as to the flagship Bordeaux blend, Angels III.

Angels Gate started as a relatively small producer, but has grown to 12,600 cases. Many have won awards, and its notable wines include both dry and off-dry Rieslings. Spytkowsky says she's especially proud of the Riesling Süssreserve, which has proved a popular seller, and the Old Vines Chardonnay, which comes from vines planted in 1970. The varietal reds also do well, especially

Merlot and Cabernet Franc. The entry level "Red" blend has been replaced by a more mainstream Cabernet-Merlot.

The flagship wine, Angels III, is a Merlot-dominant Bordeaux blend that combines Merlot from the estate vineyards with the two Cabernets. The aim, says Spytkowsky, is to make a soft, velvety, and supple wine with some longevity. The Merlot gives it roundness, and Merlot from the Bench adds a bit more tannic structure. There are plans to add a fourth variety—Petit Verdot—to the blend, but it will still be called Angels III because the wine already has a following.

Thirty Bench Vineyard and Winery

Housed in a long, low, weathered wood structure that has a hint of the Wild West about it, Thirty Bench is different from most small wineries in that it has not one but three winemakers, each responsible for specific varietals and styles. Thomas Muckle, a physician born in England, looks after the Rieslings; Yorgos Papageorgiou, a retired McMaster University professor born in Greece, takes care of the barrel-aged reds and whites; and Frank Zeritsch, a Hamilton businessman born in Austria, makes the icewines.

Diverse in original nationality and career, they were brought together by Muckle. He had some success as an amateur winemaker in the 1970s and persuaded some partners to invest in a vineyard. Located on the Beamsville Bench, it was called the French Oak vineyard and was planted in 1980, mainly with Riesling. In 1986, Muckle was involved in founding Cave Spring Cellars, but he left that partnership in 1991 and joined Papageorgiou and Zeritsch at Thirty Bench.

Although vines had been in the ground for 10 years by then, it took until 1993 for Thirty Bench to get a winery licence. From the early 1990s, other vineyards and varieties followed, until today Thirty Bench has 68 acres (27 hectares) of vines and produces 8,500 cases of wine a year. The retail shop is surrounded by racks holding a wide range of varietals, blends, and styles. The winery has long been known as a source of excellent Rieslings,

age-worthy Chardonnays and reds, and of ice-wines that are a little less sweet than many produced elsewhere.

The winery also stands out for the care it takes with its vines. All vineyard work is done by hand, and in August there's rigorous green-harvesting to intensify the character of the remaining fruit. Thirty Bench uses no pesticides but employs fungicides when necessary to deal with vineyard diseases.

In 2005 Thirty Bench was purchased by Andrés Wines (which owns Peller Estates and Hillebrand Estates), but the company said it was committed to continuing Thirty Bench as a boutique winery producing the same range and styles as before. Moreover, Thomas Muckle and Yorgos Papageorgiou continue as winemakers.

NEW GROWTH TAKES HOLD

EastDell Estates

Named for its two founders Michael East and Susan O'Dell, EastDell is one of the more isolated-looking wineries in Beamsville. You reach it by driving along Locust Lane, and you arrive to find a modest, rustic wooden building in a forest setting. Much of the winery's estate land is Carolinian forest, and there are five kilometers of trails you can enjoy—especially if you want to walk off lunch after eating at EastDell's View Restaurant. It offers a panoramic view of rolling vineyards, Lake Ontario and, often, the Toronto skyline.

Conservation is a preoccupation of the winery, and its logo features a blue heron because a number of the birds feed from the pond on the estate. EastDell is also one of those wineries setting the pace for environmental sensitivity. Much of their land is a nature conservation area, and they have developed a wetland system. All of the waste water produced by the winery and restaurant is treated to

levels that exceed standards for drinking water, and returned to the system. They've planted more than 6,000 Carolinian trees and plants.

Like many Ontario winery-founders, EastDell's had a passion for wine, but started in unrelated careers. Michael East was an engineer who began as an amateur winemaker and worked up skills as a viticulturist, while Susan O'Dell was in marketing. For years when they lived in Toronto, they talked about owning a winery, and on trips to France thought about buying land there. Having a family made this impractical, and finally O'Dell said, "Why not look for a vineyard in Niagara? We could have this nice house, and these grapes, and once a year a winery would come and take the grapes, we'd have some left for ourselves, and our friends would come, and we'd have this nice life."

In September 1996, they bought a vineyard on the Beamsville Bench. It was planted in Vidal and Seyval Blanc, and they agreed to take the crop that year. But 1996 was, as O'Dell calls it, "the year of the rain." Ten soggy days after they took ownership of the vineyard, she says, the Seyval was picked, "and guess what? It was bad, it was *so* bad!" Soon afterwards, someone advised her, "You do understand, don't you? You've got a lifestyle here, not a living."

Three years later O'Dell and East bought a winery on land adjoining theirs, and renamed it EastDell Estates. They now had a total of 63 acres (25 hectares), two-thirds planted with grapes and most of the rest set aside as a nature reserve. The vineyards now provide the winery with about a third of the grapes it needs.

EastDell aims to make a good but limited portfolio from—in Niagara terms—a quite restricted range of varieties. Their key wines are Chardonnays, Rieslings, Gewürztraminers, and blends of Baco Noir, Gamay, Cabernet Franc, and Cabernet Sauvignon, and they've had very good results from Pinot Noir. Baco Noir retains a special place and it makes up 50 to 60 percent of the Black Cab blend, with 30 percent Cabernet Franc and the rest Cabernet Sauvignon. The Escarpment Series Pinot Noir has attracted attention, too.

Although EastDell was slow to make its mark on the wine scene in Niagara, it's now establishing itself and, for a small winery, it's well represented in the LCBO. In 2005, the winery's parent company merged with another, bringing EastDell and three other wineries (Lakeview Cellars, Thomas

THE FRAGILITY OF NEW GROWTH

& Vaughan, and Birchwood Estate Wines) under common ownership. EastDell's winemaker, Scott McGregor, says his EastDell wines are based on "where we are, what we have, what nature gives us, with an astute sense of what people want."

Hidden Bench Winery

Two other wineries are close to EastDell: Hidden Bench and Fielding Estate. Hidden Bench, scheduled to open in late 2007, is the creation of Harald Thiel, an entrepreneur who sold his business in 2004 to invest in a winery. He bought two vineyards totalling 61 acres (24 hectares), one of which is the prestigious Rosomel Vineyard. This 26-acre (10-hectare) vineyard was planted in 1975, making it one of the oldest on the Beamsville Bench, and it has provided grapes for award-winning wines made by wineries like Vineland, Fielding, and Legends. It was the source of the grapes for Vineland Estate's 1998 Meritage, which sold for the then-staggering price of $125 a bottle.

Harald Thiel is another new player on Ontario's wine scene who's driven by a simple passion for wine. He grew up in a family where wine was on the table with every meal, and his grandfather in Germany had an extensive cellar. Educated in Europe, he travelled widely and explored many of the world's wine regions. He has a particular passion for Pinot Noir, and that will be the focus of Hidden Bench, although he'll make Chardonnay and Bordeaux red blends, too. (His vines include five Bordeaux red varieties.)

Thiel aims to create a small-volume winery, making 7,000 to 8,000 cases a year once Hidden Bench is in full swing. The winery's first vintage was 2003, when Thiel produced Riesling, Chardonnay and Meritage, and he's convinced he can make world-class wines from his vines. Others share his optimism. Thiel is amazed that well before his winery is slated to open—and even though he tried to keep fairly quiet about it—he received many enquiries from people wanting to make sure they're on the list to receive Hidden Bench wine when it's released. To make the wines, Thiel has been joined by Jean-Martin Bouchard, a Québecois who trained in Australia and has also worked in British Columbia. In the vineyards his consultant will be Roman Prydatkewycz, who owned the Rosomel Vineyard.

Fielding Estate Winery

Just around the corner lies Fielding Estate, where the principals are two people from the fast-food business, a car mechanic, and a professional stock-car racer. It could be the start of a bad joke but, in fact, it's the dream-team that began one of Niagara's newest and most promising wineries.

Fielding Estate is the child of Ken and Marg Fielding, who are in the fast-food business. It's an unlikely background, even in an industry, like wine, that attracts people from many different professions—until you realize that there's no reason you shouldn't enjoy a glass of quality wine with a tasty

submarine sandwich, too. The Fieldings had a passion for wine, and when they located a suitable vineyard on the Beamsville Bench, they bought it and opened their winery in the summer of 2005. Before the winery was built, the vines on the site had an excellent view of Lake Ontario and, thanks to the Fieldings' building their winery here, we can share the view. On a clear day, you can see the Toronto skyline across the shimmering water, and the vista from Fielding Estate's tasting room and shop is picture perfect.

If fast food seems like an unlikely background for a winery owner, how about a winemaker who started as an auto mechanic? Fielding Estate's Andrzej Lipinski worked on cars in Poland before immigrating to Canada in 1989 and then made a living as a construction worker before following his nose into winemaking. He started at Vineland Estates, where he made award-winning Chardonnays, like the 1998 reserve that was awarded a gold medal at Vinitaly and the 2002 that was named best Chardonnay in Ontario. From Vineland Estates, Lipinski moved to Legends Estate Winery close to Lake Ontario, before migrating up to the Fielding winery on the Bench in 2004.

Lipinski is assisted by Curtis Fielding, Ken and Marg Fielding's son, and another member of the team whose path to wine began in an unlikely place. Curtis Fielding was a professional stock-car racer who decided to trade the throttle for the bottle. He has taken courses in viticulture and winemaking, and also works on the management side of the winery operations.

It's the final member of the Fielding Estate team who sticks out—because he has a background in wine. Duarte Oliveira grew up in a Portuguese grape-growing family in Beamsville. He left the area long enough to study agriculture at the University of Guelph, but was drawn back to Beamsville and grapes. Now he manages the Fielding Estate vineyards, which include Riesling, Chardonnay, Pinot Noir, Syrah, and Cabernet Sauvignon.

Curtis Fielding refers to Andrzej, Duarte, and himself as "the three amigos," and they personify the link he makes between stock-car racing and

SUNSET ACROSS THE VINEYARDS

winemaking: both need teamwork to succeed. It seems to be working at Fielding Estate. The first vintage, 2002, produced some stylish wines, among them a 50-50 Cabernet Sauvignon-Merlot blend. The 2002 vintage was very good for reds and the Fielding blend, which was aged for 16 months in French barrels, is characterized by opulent fruit and rich complexity and has good cellaring potential.

There's a good consistent style across the portfolio, and Fielding is well worth a visit. Call in at the right time of year and you can taste the wine while sitting in one of their trademark Muskoka chairs (one appears on the Fielding label, too) and look out at the lake beyond the vines that produced the wine you're sipping.

Mountain Road Wine Company

Back down to King Street, then up Mountain Street to the Mountain Road Wine Company, and you're in no doubt you're at a working winery. On your right are the winery buildings, surrounded by pieces of working and non-working equipment: a tractor, some presses, and assorted tools. On the left is the grey brick home of the owner, Steve Kocsis, with its roofline reminiscent of the French Renaissance. The retail store and rooms hold some overflow tanks and barrels, and are part of the house.

Steve is part of the Kocsis clan who pop up here and there in Niagara's wine world. Peter Kocsis, his cousin, owns Crown Bench winery and another cousin, Thomas, founded Thomas & Vaughan. The Kocsis family fled Hungary in 1956, lived in Montreal for two years, and then came to Niagara, where Steve Kocsis's father bought land in Beamsville, including part of the present Mountain Road Winery property.

ICEWINE GRAPES

At first it was a mixed fruit farm, but Steve Kocsis planted Chardonnay, Gamay, and Vidal vines in 1983 and started selling the grapes to wineries. "We've supplied grapes to just about everyone," he says, listing most of the wineries in existence in the '80s. Mountain Road still sells about half of its fruit to other wineries, including Chardonnay to Tawse, the new high-end winery farther east along the Bench.

Steve is positive about Tawse. He admires owner Moray Tawse's commitment to quality, and contrasts him to (unnamed) "carpetbaggers" who have recently entered the industry. He marvels at Tawse winemaker Deborah Paskus' ruthless crop thinning. Standing in his vineyard in July, Kocsis points to vines laden with small green Chardonnay grapes and says, "By the time Paskus' crew come through and do a green harvest, you're ankle-deep in grapes. Look at this vine. She'd keep this bunch here, this one, she'd get rid of all these."

But grower-buyer relationships aren't always easy, and it was a problem with one of the big wineries that led Steve Kocsis to start making his own wine. In 1999 he was selling 6,000 litres of icewine juice to one of the big producers, but the Brix (sugar level) was unusually high, and the winery wanted to reduce the price they'd pay. Rather than accept the lower price, Kocsis vinified the juice himself. The result, 1999 Mountain Road Vidal Icewine, won several prizes and is sold in the LCBO's Vintages stores. Since then, he's made wine from half of his crop and sold half to other wineries.

A number of his wines are vineyard designated, several as the "Steve Kocsis Hillside Drive Vineyard" or "Steve Kocsis Mountain Road Vineyard." He's unabashed at naming the vineyard after himself: "Part of the terroir is the poor guy who sits on the tractor all day." The poor guy in this case looks after three vineyards: the one at the winery, another (Hillside Drive) also on the Beamsville Bench, and a third on the top of the escarpment where it slopes back and faces south, unlike the north-facing Bench vineyards. This third vineyard is planted with hybrids (Vidal, Baco Noir, and Maréchal Foch, and some Concord, which he sells for juice). Hybrids do better on south-facing slopes, Kocsis says, and he gets riper concentration from the Baco and Foch there.

Steve Kocsis exudes a vigneron's passion for his wines and his land. He's anxious to talk about the soil structure that makes his vineyards special, but he points out that his entire 45 acres (18 hectares) on the Bench are within the urban boundaries of Lincoln and designated for residential use. He recoils at the thought of houses being built on the stony, heavy clay soil that makes his vines struggle and gives his Chardonnay distinctive mineral notes. "I'm absolutely committed to growing grapes on subdivision land, because it's the best use of the land."

The farmer's attachment to land is evident, but Kocsis's career might well have gone in a different direction. In his early 20s, he went off to Paris to write novels and short stories and, following in the footsteps of Ernest Hemingway, spent a year "writing, drinking, and carousing." But he started to run short of francs and, having no work permit, went to Burgundy to join the thousands of seasonal workers. He did a harvest in Volnay and "developed a taste for French wine."

He evidently developed a taste for growing grapes and making wine, too. "I try to make wine in the traditional European style," he says. "But I'm also Hungarian and I like spicy food, so I want to make full-bodied wines that will stand up to it." Niagara College oenology graduate Jon Witkowski and Steve share winemaking duties. "I set the direction and Jon does most of the work to get us there. He has an amazing palate and is meticulous about winemaking. I hired him as a co-op student, and he has grown to be an enormous asset."

His wines show their style clearly. The Rieslings, which come in four styles, from dry to sweet, are well defined and show excellent varietal character. His Chardonnays are very impressive, whether unoaked, barrel-fermented, or barrel-aged. Across vintages, they're big-boned with quite intense fruit. The reds are big and fruit-forward, too. His wine sales are slower than he'd like, and he's selling four vintages behind, so the reds have a little age on them and have settled in nicely. There's a Mountain Road Red that has equal parts of Maréchal Foch, Baco Noir, Gamay, Cabernet Sauvignon, and Cabernet Franc. It's full bodied, fruity and savoury, with drying tannins. A Cabernet Sauvignon is all complex dark fruit, and a Cabernet Franc shows all the flavours you want from the variety, together with soft texture.

His successful wines from 2001 show why consumers shouldn't shy away from that vintage in Niagara, even though much of it (especially on the Beamsville Bench) was tainted by ladybug. The Mountain Road reds for sale are clean, but all that year's Gamay was affected, and Kocsis discarded it. He did bottle one 2001 Riesling, even though it was tainted and gives off the unmistakable bitter peanut flavour. It's labelled with a picture of a ladybug and is available for tasting and purchase. Reaction to the wine has been mixed, Kocsis says. "Some people love it, some people hate it."

It looks as if the Kocsis name will continue to be associated with wine in Niagara. Richard, Steve's son, gave up a comedy performance writing course ("That's all the family needed, another damned clown," Steve says) to take the viticulture and oenology course at Niagara College. "He takes visitors on tours of our vineyards. They come back and seem to have enjoyed themselves. I don't know what he tells them." Steve Kocsis, laconic, bearded, and dressed for the tractor, says his daughter Joanna and retail staff "try to keep me out of sight, because I'm not very presentable." You can take Steve Kocsis out of the Left Bank, it seems, but you can't take the Bohemian streak out of him.

Crown Bench Estates Winery

Two minutes farther on, another Kocsis, Peter, runs Crown Bench Estates winery. Like his cousin Steve, Peter is a former grape grower who decided to make his own wine rather than sell his fruit to another winery, and his winery is also new, having

BARRELS AND TANKS FOR FERMENTATION AND AGING

OPPOSITE: **SUN AND GRAPES**

opened only in 2000. But Crown Bench has a few distinctive characteristics. Its vineyards include some of the oldest vinifera vines in the area. There's a block of Chardonnay planted in 1970 that contributes the grapes for two premium Chardonnays. And Crown Bench has innovated in producing an unusual range of infused icewines. Purists might (and do) raise their eyebrows, but the wines have a real following.

Peter Kocsis is the kind of person who's sometimes described as being "his own man." He's a fierce individualist (he refers to "my somewhat skeptical nature") who distrusts many of the institutions in the wine industry ("an unbelievable bureaucracy") and wants to be left alone to grow his grapes and make his wine.

He bought the 25-acre (10-hectare) farm in 1995, when it had 10 acres (four hectares) of grapes, and began to supply wineries like Thirty Bench and Inniskillin. Some of the wines made with his grapes began to win medals, "and that set the imagination going." He stopped selling his grapes and started making his own in 1998. "So far so good," he says, reflecting on the more than 50 medals his wines have won. Crown Bench is a 100-percent estate winery, using only grapes grown in their vineyards and buying none from other growers. "That's the control on quality," says Kocsis.

Kocsis sees the Niagara wine industry splitting and heading in two different directions: quality wines and wines with mass-market appeal. "It bothers me," he says. He's not interested in competing for the mass market, but aims at a higher end with winemaking techniques that take time. His top reds go through a two-week cold maceration, then a cool, slow fermentation, and then two years in barrels. When they're bottled, he says, they need at least another year before you think of drinking them.

What that means is that they don't necessarily show well when they're young, and Kocsis says he's noticed an inverse relationship between the scores wines get at the VQA testing: the lower the score (that is, the closer they are to failing), the better they do as medal-winners. The difficulty is to see where a raw wine is going to go, and too often, Kocsis says, "a young tannic, bite-you-in-the-side-of-the-cheeks" sort of wine is downgraded, whereas the judges ought to be going in the other direction. He's also irked by wine competitions that restrict entrants to wines one or two years old, because some of his wines won't show well for four years.

Like a lot of winery owners, Kocsis is concerned about the opportunities for sales. He's resigned to not getting his wines into the LCBO, but chafes that he can't open a private store. He'd like to be able to sell his wine at places like Toronto's St. Lawrence Market and Ottawa's By Ward Market. "I can make the best wine in the world," he says, "but it's no good if I can't sell it." There's a retail shop at his winery, which is at the end of an unpaved road off King Street, but "casual kibitzers don't come up this

road. You have to want to find me. It's all very well to sell to people on wine tours, but you have to get the people down here." How many people, he asks, have the time to come to wineries all the time?

Among Crown Bench's sweet wines, a notable is Livia's Gold, named for Peter Kocsis's wife and the winery's president. In 2002, the 2000 vintage won a gold medal at the prestigious International Wine and Spirits Competition in London. It's a botrytis-affected late-harvest Chardonnay in the Sauternes style, and Kocsis would like to plant Semillon to see how that does. As for those infused icewines, they come in several styles. Ambrosia is infused with chocolate, Hot Ice is flavoured with jalapeño peppers, and Altair is given a Canadian spin with maple syrup. There are also three berry-infused icewines (blueberry, raspberry, and cranberry) and one that blends all three.

De Sousa Wine Cellars
Some distance along Quarry Road, which runs parallel to Mountain Road up the Beamsville Bench to the Escarpment, is De Sousa Wine Cellars. Housed in a distinctly bodega-style building, two storeys high and with a flat roofline and wrought-iron balconies on the upper level, it's one of Niagara's lower-profile wineries. De Sousa sells most of its table wines in large formats (including a 16-litre bag-in-box) on the Toronto market, but it makes a fair volume of port-style wine and has also started to produce some reserve-level wines.

The port reflects the origins of the winery, which was opened in the early 1980s by John De Sousa, who emigrated from Portugal to Canada in 1961. His father had made a living in Portugal by supplying wine to bars, using a horse and cart. In recognition of the family's origins, a cart bearing two barrels stands in front of the winery. John De Sousa started out in the wine business in 1979 by buying 22 acres (nine hectares) of land for vines, and later added neighbouring vineyards to make the current 85 acres (34 hectares). He died in 1997, and his son, also named John, now runs the winery.

De Sousa's vines are both hybrids and vinifera, and include the Portuguese vinifera Touriga Nacional. Transplanted from the sun-baked terraces of the Douro River Valley, the Touriga Nacional vines need to be buried during the Ontario winters. They're the basis of De Sousa Port, which is made in the ruby style. Eventually, Port-style wine will no longer be called "port" unless it's made in Portugal's Douro Valley. John De Sousa speculates that he might call his wines *abafado* (Portuguese for "fortified") or *forte*.

The bestselling of De Sousa's 20,000 cases of wine is called "Dois Amigos" ("Two Friends"), after the two winemakers who worked on the first vintage. Like the Port, it sells well among Toronto's big Portuguese community. To take advantage of the Toronto market, De Sousa opened a winery on Dundas Street ("the only winery in the heart of Toronto," De Sousa says) in 1998.

Since 2001, De Sousa has been making a reserve line of wines in a less Portuguese, more mainstream European style. For this purpose, he hired Andrzej Lipinski (now winemaker at Fielding Estate Winery) as a consultant. His reserves include Chardonnay, Cabernet Franc, Cabernet-Merlot, and Merlot.

Malivoire Wine Company
Drive off King Street near Beamsville at the sign with a red and black ladybug and you encounter a building more futuristic than historic. The Malivoire Wine Company is the creation of special effects movie director Martin Malivoire, who started visiting Niagara in the 1970s when he thought "it was pretty neat that we had a wine region" near Toronto. In those days there weren't many vinifera wines, but the idea kept him going. The love affair wasn't entirely reciprocated. In the summer of 1990, Malivoire made a movie in Niagara-on-the-Lake and dumped 75,000 pounds of potato flakes in the street to simulate snow. The city passed a by-law forbidding their use after that.

Malivoire says that moving to Niagara was a lifestyle decision—to have a home in wine country—but his decisions point to the importance of wine. He started looking for land from 1990, first in Niagara-on-the-Lake, then in Beamsville. "Niagara-on-the-Lake looked good for lifestyle, but

Beamsville looked better for grapes." He bought a vineyard in 1995 (it's now called the Moira Vineyard, for his wife and winery partner) and sold most of his first harvest to wineries, keeping a small batch for himself. He was convinced he could get better results from other grape varieties, so he ripped out most of the mature vines and replanted in Chardonnay and Pinot Noir.

He was also sure that the wine he made was better than the wine that others were making with his grapes, and he decided to go for broke and start his own winery. "I don't think anyone believed me when I said, 'I think I'll just start building it.'" In 1997 he bought the land where the winery is now located.

Many of the most successful small wineries in Ontario are partnerships of passionate entrepreneurs and skilled winemakers, and in the winter of 1997–98, Martin Malivoire met his future partner in wine, Ann Sperling. Sperling was making wine in

Niagara when Malivoire met her, and he began to talk about how wine should ideally be made. "Ann corrected me," he says, "which is the way things have usually gone since."

They met when Sperling tasted some batches of Gewürztraminer that Malivoire had made, some as late-harvest dry wine, some as late-harvest dessert wine, some as icewine. Sperling says she "went away thinking 'this is the best Gewürztraminer I've tasted in Niagara, certainly, and Canada as well, so there was something there in the vineyard that was worth looking at.'" In 1999, wine from one of those batches won a gold medal in the Best Single Estate Icewine/Eiswein category at the International Wine and Spirits Competition in London.

The Malivoire Wine Company is housed in an extended set of stacked Quonset huts, structures

DISCS TO DETER BIRDS

EVIDENCE OF THE PROXIMITY OF LAKE ONTARIO

designed for the U.S. Navy during World War II. Quonset huts are made of semicircular steel ribs covered with corrugated sheet metal, and Malivoire's are built on a 30-foot hillside that was too steep for vines. The design might be more than half a century old, but it looks thoroughly modern. At first it was bright red and, says Malivoire, "You could see it from everywhere, like this giant strawberry sticking out of the Bench. So I painted it camouflage green. Now if you look at it, it looks like rows of grapes on a hill. I think that's pretty neat."

This ingenious use of land enabled Malivoire to build a winery on several levels. The grapes are crushed on the top level, and each major stage in the operation is on a lower level, with the barrel room and bottling line on the ground floor. This gravity-fed system is a much more gentle way of treating juice and wine than pumping them under pressure from one stage of production to another.

Malivoire has three vineyards, one (called the Estate vineyard) around the winery itself. It's planted with Chardonnay, Pinot Noir, Pinot Gris, Gamay, and Gewürztraminer. A kilometre away is the original Moira Vineyard with its Chardonnay and Pinot Noir vines. A third vineyard grows the Maréchal Foch vines, planted in 1975, that produce Malivoire's Old Vines Foch.

One of the distinctive characteristics of the Malivoire winery is that it uses no pesticides or herbicides and is moving toward organic certification. This not only requires a winery to eliminate pesticides and herbicides but also to cultivate its vines that way for three years. Nor can there be any risk of chemical spill-over (like spray carried on the wind) from neighbouring non-organic vineyards.

Malivoire's Moira Vineyard, which produces one of its best-known and most popular Chardonnays, has been certified organic since the 2004 vintage. Martin Malivoire argues that organic farming isn't only philosophically better, but results in healthier vines that grow more slowly. Ann Sperling credits it with producing plants with denser wood that weathered the harsh winter of 2002–03 much better than vines in non-organic vineyards.

Even so, they're mindful that consumers sometimes shy away from organic wines because they think they might have a short shelf life or think they're made with some "biodynamic hocus-pocus," and there are no plans to advertise Malivoire wines as organic. "We'll let people taste the wines, and if they like them, and want to know more about them, that's fine," says Malivoire. Ann Sperling points out that "organic" means different things in different countries, which makes it tricky for consumers.

Like most wineries, Malivoire uses deterrents to deal with pests like birds and deer, but they go further than most in dealing naturally with other insect problems. In a well-publicized episode, Malivoire introduced thousands of ladybugs (of an indigenous variety, unlike the Asian strain that caused the problem in 2001) into their vineyard to deal with leaf-hoppers.

There's a difference between organically grown grapes and organically made wine. As far as the wine-making at Malivoire is concerned, as much as possible is natural, and intervention is kept to a minimum. They use wild yeasts, and although the whites are fined with bentonite, they're only coarse-filtered. The reds aren't fined or filtered at all.

Martin Malivoire no longer makes as many movies as he used to; from 10 a year in his heyday, he's down to one. Now he's the director of The Malivoire Wine Company, and spends most of his time there, more in the vineyards than the winery. Ann Sperling, his star winemaker since the winery opened in 1999, was named Niagara's Winemaker of the Year in 2004. She has now moved into an advisory role at Malivoire and continues to contribute to the winery's stylistic plan. Other leading players are Shiraz Mottiar, who was appointed winemaker in 2005, and vineyard manager Dave Crowe.

Unlike many Niagara wineries, Malivoire decided early on to restrict its production to a small number of grape varieties. Martin Malivoire saw similarities between his land and vineyards in Burgundy and Alsace, so Pinot Noir, Chardonnay, and Gamay (all Burgundy grapes) were naturals, as were Pinot

TILLING THE EARTH BETWEEN THE ROWS

Gris and Gewürztraminer from Alsace. Added to those are Maréchal Foch, a hybrid that does well in Niagara, and some Cabernet Sauvignon and Merlot. Styles include red, white, and rosé table wines, late harvest and icewine. They also buy some grapes, including Cabernet Franc for their rosé.

A recent addition to the range is Melon de Bourgogne, the signature grape of the Muscadet region at the Atlantic end of France's Loire Valley. Muscadet is one of the most popular seafood wines in France, and Malivoire sells its zesty, citrus-flavoured Melon as "Martin's oyster wine." It has become one of *those* wines, and the 50 cases sell within a couple of days of the wine's release. There's also a vin gris, a light-coloured wine made from Pinot Noir. Malivoire and Sperling travelled to Ottawa in 2005 to do the blending exercise with

WINTER PRUNING

a group of wine enthusiasts and professionals at one of the city's restaurants, and the wine was sold exclusively there when it was released in late 2005.

Overall, Malivoire aims to restrict its portfolio to the grapes that do best in its vineyards and to continue to improve those varieties. "There are many varieties we're not making," says Sperling, "but you can spread yourself too thin and lose out. It's a greater challenge to continue to make wine better than it is to make more." Malivoire and Sperling are pinning their hopes on Pinot Noir. Their Chardonnay (especially Moira's Chardonnay) has won wide acclaim but, Sperling says, "it's Pinot Noir that will firmly establish us here." Along with the select range of grapes, Malivoire believes in limited production. In the early 2000s they produced about 9,000 cases a year, and Martin Malivoire can't see increasing that beyond 14,000, even though the winery has a capacity of 20,000 cases a year.

Thomas & Vaughan

On the other side of King Street, on the plain that runs from the base of the Beamsville Bench to the lake, is the modest structure of Thomas & Vaughan. It was founded by Thomas Kocsis and Barbara Vaughan who, like many winery owners, began as grape growers before deciding to make their own wine. They made their first vintage in 1997 and opened to the public in 1999. Thomas & Vaughan quickly established a reputation for their Bordeaux reds, particularly the Cabernet Francs, with the reserve Cabernet Francs winning accolades consistently; some, like the 1999 vintage, stand out among the best produced in the region. There are strong whites, too, like the Chardonnays aged for a year in American or French oak. The vines are more than 30 years old and produce wines with good structure and complexity.

Thomas Kocsis, who is no longer involved in the winery, attributed the success of his reds partly to the superior fruit produced in the heavy red clay soil. The soil is so dense, Kocsis said, that it took three attempts to get some of the vines to take root, and he kept yields low. They produce small berries with intense flavours. On the vinification side, Kocsis was big on barrel-aging. The 1999 Reserve Cabernet Franc spent 24 months in oak, the 2000 vintage got six months more, and in neither case did the wood dull the fruit's vibrancy.

Kocsis also did well with Baco Noir and Maréchal Foch, and he never shied away from hybrids, which have a following among consumers. "It'll be a sad day when there's nothing but Cabernet Sauvignon and Merlot all over the world," he said, "so hybrids have a place at Thomas & Vaughan as long as the quality is good." There was even a small parcel of Catawba, a labrusca variety, in the vineyard, and for a few years Kocsis used it to make a funky dessert wine called "Old Gold." But the vines were sacrificed to make way for new plantings, which included Syrah and Merlot. He wasn't sure about the future of Pinot Noir in the region and decided against planting any.

In 2005, Thomas & Vaughan merged with the company that also owns EastDell Estates,

Birchwood Estate Wines, and Lakeview Cellars. A new winemaker, Scott McGregor, joined Thomas & Vaughan, and continues the winemaking practices of former winemaker, Jason James. There are no plans to alter the winery's position as a producer of small volumes of premium wines.

Birchwood Estate Wines

One of Thomas & Vaughan's new sibling wineries, Birchwood Estate, is located closer to the lakeshore, not far from the Queen Elizabeth Way. Birchwood opened in 2000 on the site that had been occupied by Willow Heights winery, where visitors will find a small cottage-style winery, not too far off the beaten path. The 10-acre (four-hectare) vineyard benefits from a good flow of warm air that deals effectively with moisture among the vines and produces up to 5,000 cases of wine a year. The wine is actually made at Lakeview Estates, by winemaker Tom Green.

For Birchwood, Green focuses on producing well-made, straightforward, affordable wines for early drinking. Of the white wines in its portfolio, only the Chardonnay sees any oak, while all the reds get a little barrel-aging. Barrels are expensive, and by minimizing their use, the winery is able to sell its wines at relatively low prices. Recent vintages of its crisp, aromatic Gewürztraminer-Riesling blend have been very well received. A Salmon River line of wines was launched in 2003, with the expectation of creating a brand that consumers will easily remember. The first release was a rosé, and it was followed by two blends: Cabernet-Merlot and Pinot Gris-Chardonnay. The core Birchwood Estate line-up has a wide range of table wines, as well as dessert styles. Some have done well in competitions, and the 2000 Baco Noir won Best Red Hybrid in Canada at the Canadian Wine Awards.

A VINEYARD IN FULL LEAF

Royal DeMaria Wines

A little farther inland from Birchwood Estates is Ontario's only winery dedicated to the production of icewine. It's named for the founder, hairdresser Joseph DeMaria, who tasted icewine for the first time in 1991. It seemed to move the earth for him,

BUDS FORMING

and five years later he bought a 25-acre (10-hectare) vineyard, and started selling icewine juice to wineries. Then in 1998, like several other grape growers, he found himself with excess juice on his hands (5,000 litres in his case) and decided to make his own wine. It was a move "from coiffure to terroir."

Producing wine in only one style was a real gamble, but DeMaria had faith in the future of icewine as a luxury product that would find markets in the same way as other luxury products. Although his production is all icewine, he has diversified his portfolio by using a wider range of grape varieties than any other single producer. DeMaria currently produces icewines made from more than 16 varieties and blends. They include Vidal and Riesling, Niagara's workhorse icewine grapes,

and also Gamay, Pinot Blanc, Muscat Ottonel, Gewürztraminer, and Pinot Gris. There are also sparkling icewines.

Prices start at about $60 for 375-mL bottles, but because Joseph DeMaria is convinced that prices ought to reflect the value of his luxury products, he hasn't hesitated to charge high prices for vintages and varieties that are almost exhausted. Royal DeMaria's Collectors Series comprises icewines that were originally produced in commercial quantities, but are now down to five cases (60 bottles) or less. The series includes 2000 Pinot Gris Icewine, which sells for $2,500 a bottle, and 2000 Chardonnay Icewine, priced at $2,000. But the most expensive icewine (not only at the Royal DeMaria winery, but in the world) is Royal DeMaria's 2002 Meritage Icewine, the first made from this red blend. It originally went on sale for $395 a bottle, but once stocks fell to five cases (from the 33 cases made), he re-priced it at a cool $5,000 a bottle.

Joseph DeMaria isn't shy about promoting his products. He has registered the trademark, "Canada's Icewine Specialists" for his winery, and it has been referred to as "the Versace of icewine." He also points out the celebrities who have ordered his wine, including Queen Elizabeth II and Sir Richard Branson. Then again, who can deny the success of his wines in prestigious international competitions? There are dozens of medals, and at the 2002 Citadelles du Vin competition in Bordeaux, Royal DeMaria picked up five gold trophies, a record.

Magnotta Winery Corporation

A few kilometres from Royal DeMaria, but an infinity away in style, is the Magnotta Winery Corporation. The "Winery Corporation" tag makes Magnotta sound like a high-volume, impersonal producer, and the first impression of the company's retail store just off the Queen Elizabeth Way seems to confirm it. Far from the small boutiques at many Ontario wineries, it's set out like a supermarket, and shoppers are provided with carts they can load up with bottles and bag-in-boxes.

Magnotta is, though, a winery with a varied face. It makes high-volume, inexpensive wines—millions of litres of them a year. Some are 100-percent Ontario fruit; some are blends of Ontario and imported wines. Much of the imported wine comes from Magnotta's own 350-acre (140-hectare) vineyard in Chile's Maipo Valley. In all, Magnotta produces about 3.8 million litres of wine, the equivalent of 420,000 cases, each year. That total includes between 30,000 and 40,000 cases of VQA wine, produced from Magnotta's 180 acres (72 hectares) of vines in Niagara. The main 120-acre (48-hectare) vineyard is on Merritt Road near Lake Ontario; two more are located in Niagara-on-the-Lake, and the last is on top of the escarpment. Grape varieties planted include Riesling, Pinot Gris, Sauvignon Blanc, Chardonnay, Pinot Noir, and the three main Bordeaux reds.

The Magnotta winery was launched in 1989 by Rossana and Gabriel Magnotta. She was a laboratory technologist, who transferred her skills in chemistry to amateur winemaking, and he was a businessman. After working with other home winemakers, the Magnottas bought a failing winery, Charal, and subsequently acquired several more. In little time they expanded the business to include not only wine but also beer, distilled spirits, and grape juice for home winemakers. Magnotta is now listed on the Toronto Stock Exchange.

The Magnotta range is enormous. There are 180 different products, ranging from vodka and grappa, through sparkling, fruit, and fortified wines, to a wide selection of white, rosé, red table, and dessert wines. About 60 of the products are VQA-classified. The winery has developed several new products, some in icewine, through which it has carved out a name for itself. Magnotta was one of the first to produce sparkling icewine, in 1997, and the first and only to make icewine grappa. This is made by fermenting the skins and other residue left after icewine grapes are pressed, and then twice-distilling the result. Called Icegrappa, it has 45 percent alcohol. More recently, the winery distilled icewine into an eau-de-vie called Primissimo. It takes 20 bottles of icewine to make one of Primissimo, and the price tag reflects it: sold in a crystal bottle and described as "the most expensive non-aged spirit ever," it's priced at $1,500—but that's for a 750-mL bottle, twice the size of the usual icewine bottle.

Icewine is a major component of Magnotta's VQA production, and the distinctive blue bottle with its red and white Canadian flag label stands out at the winery and on LCBO shelves. Magnotta and the LCBO went through a stormy period in the late 1990s, culminating in the Magnotta's filing a claim for $8 million, but the case was settled out of court. Although few Magnotta wines grace LCBO shelves, the icewine sells well there.

Their flagship wine is Enotrium, a blend of Merlot, Cabernet Sauvignon, and Cabernet Franc that's made in the Amarone style, where the grapes are allowed to dry for a period before they're pressed. The result is a high-alcohol, intensely flavoured wine. Rossana Magnotta says they decided to make it as a response to a challenge. "Our family and friends in Italy think no one can out-do Italian wines, so we took up the challenge, and with the right grapes and the proper skills, we made Enotrium. Now they're impressed that Canada can make such wine. We have a lot of pride in that one." Enotrium is made in small batches from selected grapes. The first vintage was 2001, and the 1,800 bottles sold out in three months. In 2002, production rose to 2,400 bottles. This vintage also sold well and can be found in some high-end Toronto restaurants.

The Magnottas have no reservations about blending Ontario and foreign wine. Rossana Magnotta says it's necessary in order to pay the bills when the weather produces short crops of local grapes; it keeps wineries in business, and overall it's good for the Ontario wine industry. The Magnottas draw much of their non-Ontario fruit from their own vineyards in Chile, which they bought to give themselves some flexibility when the Ontario weather lets them down. Besides, Rossana Magnotta says, "We can say, 'This is from our vineyard in Chile and from our vineyard in Ontario.' It gives customers confidence in what they're getting, and keeps them interested in Ontario wine." It can also make for interesting blends, such as the addition of Carmenère, Chile's signature grape variety.

Rossana Magnotta is optimistic about the future of her winery and the success of Ontario wine generally. She and Gabriel Magnotta look like the first generation of a wine dynasty. Their three children are showing interest in the wine industry, and even though this is a public company, the Magnotta family is at its centre. Rossana Magnotta highlights this: "A member of the Magnotta family has to taste and approve every batch of wine before it's released."

Legends Estate Winery

Across the Queen Elizabeth Way, close to the shore of Lake Ontario is Legends Estate Winery, named for an aspiration—that its wines will become legends—and for its history. Legends is the present incarnation of a property established by John Lizak in 1946 as a fruit orchard. Sixty years later, his grandson, Paul Lizak, farms about 200 acres (80 hectares) of fruit trees and 50 acres (20 hectares) of grapevines. The winery grew out of the orchard almost by chance. Paul Lizak and his father, Ted, began to make wine from the fruit that wasn't cosmetically good enough for the market. From mastering fruit wines, it was a short step to planting grapes and making wine. Legends still produces both fruit and grape wines, with the grape wine accounting for three-quarters of production and increasing its share.

The first wines were made by Paul Lizak, with Jim Warren as consultant. Andrzej Lipinski, who is now at Fielding Estate winery, then came on board. On his watch, Legends fared well in wine competitions, the 2002 whites and reds picking up awards in Canada, the United States, and Europe. His notable wines include complex Chardonnays, fruity Pinot Gris, and Cabernet Francs that confirm its status as one of Niagara's best varieties. His 2002 Pinot Noir stands out as one of Niagara's best that year.

Lipinski left in 2004 and his place was taken by Andreea Botezatu, an oenologist from Romania. She arrived at Legends just in time to do the 2004 crush, and made some very good whites from the vintage. Now, Paul Lizak is back making the wines. He describes himself as self taught, but says he learned from Warren, Lipinski, and Botezatu: "They're all

different winemakers and had different strengths." He's impressed that the winery has maintained a consistent style throughout and says you can see it if you compare the Chardonnays from 2002, 2003, and 2004. He aims to follow the trajectory but to stress Old World styles with complexity and structure, rather than wines that are made table-ready.

VINES AND ESCARPMENT
OPPOSITE: **HOSING DOWN THE EQUIPMENT**

As he sees it, his market reflects the multicultural character of the region, and people are looking for wines that have more than fruit.

Legends produced 15,000 cases of wine in 2004, but the volume shrank to half that in 2005, as it did for most Niagara Peninsula wineries. Still, Lizak is optimistic and is thinking about new varieties like Malbec, Petit Verdot, and Semillon. But he'll see what the climate deals him and will tailor his wines to the conditions of each vintage.

THE WINERIES

Angels Gate Winery
4260 Mountainview Road
Beamsville, ON L0R 1B2
Tel: 905-563-3942
www.angelsgatewinery.com

Birchwood Estate Wines
4679 Cherry Avenue
Beamsville, ON L0R 1B1
Tel: 905-562-8463
www.birchwoodwines.ca

Crown Bench Estates Winery
3850 Aberdeen Road
Beamsville, ON L0R 1B7
Tel: 888-537-6192
www.crownbenchestates.com

Daniel Lenko Estate Winery
5246 Regional Road 81
Beamsville, ON L0R 1B3
Tel: 905-563-7756
www.daniellenko.com

De Sousa Wine Cellars
3753 Quarry Road
Beamsville, ON L0R 1B0
Tel: 905-563-7269

802 Dundas Street West
Toronto, ON M6J 1V3
Tel: 416-603-0202
www.desousawines.com

EastDell Estates
4041 Locust Lane
Beamsville, ON L0R 1B2
Tel: 905-563-9463
www.eastdell.com

Fielding Estate Winery
4020 Locust Lane
Beamsville, ON L0R 1B2
Tel: 905-563-0668
www.fieldingwines.com

Hidden Bench Vineyards & Winery
4152 Locust Lane
Beamsville, ON L0R 1B2
Tel: 905-563-8700
www.hiddenbench.com

Kittling Ridge Estate Wines & Spirits
297 South Service Road
Grimsby, ON L3M 1Y6
Tel: 905-945-9225
www.kittlingridge.com

Legends Estates Winery
4888 Ontario Street North
Beamsville, ON L0R 1B3
Tel: 905-563-6500
www.legendsestates.com

Magnotta Winery Corporation
4701 Ontario Street
Beamsville, ON L0R 1B4
Tel: 905-563-5313

271 Chrislea Road
Vaughan, ON L4L 8N6
Tel: 905-738-9463
www.magnotta.com

Malivoire Wine Company
4260 King Street East
Beamsville, ON L0R 1B0
Tel: 905-563-9253
www.malivoirewineco.com

THE WINERIES

Mountain Road Wine Company
4016 Mountain Street
Beamsville, ON L0R 1B7
Tel: 905-563-0745
www.mountainroadwine.com

Peninsula Ridge Estates Winery
5600 King Street West
Beamsville, ON L0R 1B0
Tel: 905-563-0900
www.peninsularidge.com

Puddicombe Estate Farms & Winery
1468 Highway 8
Winona, ON L8E 5K9
Tel: 905-643-1015
www.puddicombefarms.com

Royal DeMaria Wines
4551 Cherry Avenue
Beamsville, ON L0R 1B1
Tel: 905-562-6767
www.royaldemaria.com

Thirty Bench Vineyard & Winery
4281 Mountainview Road
Beamsville, ON L0R 1B0
Tel: 905-563-1698
www.thirtybench.com

Thomas & Vaughan
4245 King Street
Beamsville, ON L0R 1B1
Tel: 905-563-7737
www.thomasandvaughan.com

NIAGARA: VINELAND, JORDAN, AND ST. CATHARINES

"WE CAN MAKE A VERY GOOD CHARDONNAY, BUT IT'S UBIQUITOUS. I WISH THE INDUSTRY WOULD GET BEHIND RIESLING THE WAY NEW ZEALAND DID WITH SAUVIGNON BLANC."

—DANIEL SPECK
HENRY OF PELHAM FAMILY ESTATE WINERY

Between Beamsville and the city of St. Catharines, the best-known wine areas are Vineland, Jordan, and St. Catharines, but in the last few years several wineries have identified themselves with the Twenty Mile Valley. The Twenty Mile Creek, like other references to "Miles" in Niagara place names, denotes the distance from Niagara Falls. In fact, the creek forms its own quite impressive falls, Balls Falls, as it tumbles over the Niagara Escarpment.

From the base of the escarpment, Twenty Mile Creek flows across a bench, dividing it into the Beamsville Bench to the west and the Jordan Bench to the east. Then the creek makes its way to Jordan Harbour, an inlet of Lake Ontario. En route, it separates the communities of Vineland and Jordan.

The recent creation of the Twenty Mile area as an identifiable wine and tourist region reorients the way we view the topography of this part of the Niagara Peninsula. It recognizes the importance of the Creek as the main waterway in the Niagara watershed and is represented in two of the new sub-appellations: Twenty Mile Bench and Creek Shores.

THE WINERIES OF VINELAND

Lakeview Cellars Estate Winery
Several wineries are clustered on each side of King Street (Regional Road 81) between Cherry Avenue

OPPOSITE: **EMBRYONIC GRAPES**

and Twenty Mile Creek, which crosses the Bench between—of course!—21st Street and 19th Street. On the Bench, up Cherry Avenue, is Lakeview Cellars, now part of the company that owns EastDell Estate, Thomas & Vaughan, and Birchwood Estate. Lakeview is the largest producer of the quartet, with about 20,000 cases a year. Its size is belied by the modest building that houses it.

Eddy and Lorraine Gurinskas bought the 13-acre (5-hectare) property in 1986, after Eddy retired from his job with CN Rail in Ottawa. He was a skilled amateur winemaker, and his friends persuaded him to buy a vineyard. For the next four years he commuted between Ottawa and Niagara almost every weekend to look after his grapes. In 1991 he moved to Niagara and opened the winery. Gurinskas adapted to commercial production, favouring the full-bodied reds for which Lakeview Cellars has become known. He took on some partners, including current vineyard manager Larry Hipple, in 1996. In 2000 Diamond Estates invested in the winery and later purchased it.

In 2003 Eddy Gurinskas was named Ontario Winemaker of the Year at the Ontario Wine Awards, and that year he passed winemaking responsibilities to Thomas Green, a graduate of Brock University's oenology and viticulture program, who had been working with Gurinskas since 1999. He has made Lakeview's wines since and continues the tradition of big reds. The 2002 vintage produced a number of concentrated, complex reds, including a Meritage, and the Baco Noir won Best Red Hybrid at Cuvée in 2005. Lakeview planted Syrah in 2001, and Green is looking forward to making wine from it. He says, "We'll wait and see what we get. But we know how to make big, full-bodied reds, and we'll play that over to the Syrah. We'd like to make it as big as we can get. Obviously it will be a cool climate variety; we're not going to shoot for the warm climate style of Shiraz."

Under Green's stewardship, the whites are gaining ground. He's keen on Riesling and Chardonnay, which have sold very well, and he'd like to plant Sauvignon Blanc. "Lakeview dabbles in a lot of interesting varieties," he says. "We make a Kerner,

a Welschriesling . . . we like to keep an interesting cottage effect." Lakeview's portfolio lists about 40 different wines. Basically, Green says, Lakeview produces enough different wines so that no one is likely to walk into the retail store and leave without a bottle.

Their extensive repertoire includes a port-style wine made from Cabernet Sauvignon. It's made from the best grapes, is VQA-certified, and has much of the flavour and layered character of very good ruby port. Like California's Quady winery, which has been making a port-style wine since the late 1980s, Lakeview calls its version (made since 1995) Starboard.

Green is a strong believer in the regional character that grapes bring to wine. Lakeview's own vineyards provide only about 15 percent of the winery's needs, and he sources the rest locally. All grow within five kilometres of Lakeview, and 90 percent come from Bench vineyards, to maintain the integrity of his wine. He says: "I wouldn't buy any from Niagara-on-the-Lake because that's their terroir."

Tawse Winery

Along Cherry Avenue is one of Ontario's impressive new wineries, Tawse Winery. It's named for owner Moray Tawse, a Toronto mortgage financier and wine lover. He started building the winery in 2002 and completed it three years later, and it sits back from the road, across a pond, looking like a majestic mansion. The high wood-shingled roof is sharply-pitched, with two long dormer windows. The winery is built against a ridge, but rises high above it so as to house winemaking facilities that are completely gravity-fed: 90 feet (27 metres) separate the floor on the bottom level from the floor on the top. At harvest, the grapes are winched to the uppermost level after being sorted, and then begin their slow progress down the six levels to end up as finished wine.

Tawse owns 32 acres (13 hectares) of vines on the winery property and another 48 acres (19 hectares) elsewhere on the Bench. They're planted with 25-year-old Chardonnay and 30-year-

PROTECTING THE RIPENING GRAPES

old Riesling, as well as younger Cabernet Franc and Chardonnay. The winery aims to produce a limited range: Pinot Noir, Chardonnay, Riesling, and Cabernet Franc, all classic French cool-climate varieties. Moray Tawse is especially focused on Pinot Noir and Chardonnay, the Burgundy grapes. He says he sees the Beamsville Bench as Niagara's Burgundy and Niagara-on-the-Lake as its Bordeaux.

Tawse's exposure to wine started when he was a server, then sommelier, at the Banff Springs Hotel. Later, he was able to expand his palate on holidays in Burgundy. The only Ontario wines he'd tasted at that time were mediocre, but then he met Deborah Paskus, one of Niagara's foremost winemakers, and tasted her Temkin Paskus Chardonnay. "It blew me away," he says. He'd been thinking of investing in a winery in France, but that one wine drove him to look at possibilities in Niagara. Deborah Paskus is now the winemaker at Tawse winery.

Taking aim at the higher end of the market, Tawse intends to make a reputation as a small-volume producer of super-premium wines. All the wines are aged 18 to 20 months in barrels and get a further nine months in the bottle before being released. Wines in the higher-quality tiers are available in both standard bottles and magnums. Production began in 2001, with the first commercial vintage the following year, which was one of Niagara's best. The current production is about 2,000 cases, and Tawse aims at a maximum of 5,000 cases a year once the winery is in full swing.

The first vintages of Tawse wines represented an impressive start. The Carly's Block Rieslings (named for one of Tawse's daughters) capture lovely fruit and entwine it with bright acidity, while the Robyn's

Block Chardonnays (another daughter) are big and rich and have much of the character often associated with red wine. The tannins are perceptible, and Tawse suggests the Chardonnay would benefit from being decanted. As for the Vintner's Reserve Pinot Noir, it offers elegant and pure fruit flavours

ADVICE TO VISITORS

with earthy notes, along with silky texture. The only shortcoming was supply: a mere 240 bottles of the 2002 vintage were made—not even a barrel-full.

Moray Tawse seems to have put everything into place in his winery. Now, he says, they have to get the grapes right, and part of that will be the simple passage of time.

Ridgepoint Wines
Located farther up Cherry Avenue, Ridgepoint Wines is the only Niagara winery to make wine from Nebbiolo, the variety responsible for many of the big reds from northern Italy. It's predictable that only a winery with owners of Italian heritage would try it. They turned out to be Mauro Scarsellone and his sister Anna, two more Torontonians (he's a chartered accountant) who gazed south across Lake

Ontario, dreamed of making wine, and followed their dream. The Scarsellones bought 20 acres (eight hectares) of land on the Bench, in what will become the Twenty Mile Bench sub-appellation, and started planting grapes in 1995. They put in nine varieties and, although the vineyard includes Chardonnay and Riesling, the stress is on red: some Pinot Noir, Cabernet Sauvignon, Merlot, and Nebbiolo. Continuing the Italian theme, they added an experimental parcel of Sangiovese in 2005.

The wines are promising and will develop as the vines age. The early vintages of Pinot Noir were light and elegant, with good fruit flavours and quite gripping tannins, while the Merlots from warm years offer big flavours of dark fruit and firm tannins. Some of the wines are made in small volumes; there were only four barrels of the 2002 Merlot.

Mauro Scarsellone presides over the counter of the tasting room like a genial barman and talks optimistically about the future of Nebbiolo in Niagara. It is, he says, "a quest and a passion." And although it's also in his heritage, he recognizes that local Nebbiolo won't be a high-alcohol bruiser of the sort that comes from the Piedmont. Ridgepoint's Nebbiolo from the warm, dry 2002 vintage came in at a surprisingly modest 12.5 percent alcohol. This was Ridgepoint's first commercial bottling of the varietal, and the vines were still only four years old. There was only one barrel of the 2001 Nebbiolo, and it sold out quickly, but there are eight barrels of the 2002 vintage. "A crop size is key," says consultant winemaker Arthur Harder. With older vines and careful attention to yield, Ridgepoint could find itself producing a cult wine.

Willow Heights Estate Winery
Below the Bench, sitting slightly below the elevation of King Street, is Willow Heights Estate Winery. The winery is housed in a building modelled on a hacienda, with a red-tile roof, stucco exterior, and a courtyard with a fountain. The vineyards slope gently away toward the lakeshore, which is about four kilometres away. Like so many Ontario wineries, this was started by an amateur winemaker with ambition. Ron Speranzini was a manager at

Stelco, the Hamilton steel company. He made wine in his spare time, won prizes, and was encouraged by his friends to start a winery. He bought what's now the Birchwood Estate Winery, made his first commercial vintage in 1992, and opened a winery in 1994. Within a few years, production outgrew the facilities, and Willow Heights moved to its present location, where it produces about 15,000 cases of wine a year.

Over time, Willow Heights has developed several signature wines. One is a luxurious Reserve Chardonnay, aged in American oak and made only in years when the grapes are deemed good enough. The other is a Bordeaux blend called Tresette, after an Italian card game. (You need a pack of 40 cards with the Italian suits: swords, batons, cups, and coins. Drinking the Willow Heights wine sounds preferable.) Speranzini also makes up to 500 cases of icewine each year. During its first decade, Willow Heights purchased most of the grapes it needed,

but in 2003 Speranzini and some partners bought a 175-acre (70-hectare) vineyard near Grimsby at the western end of the Niagara wine region.

Vineland Estates Winery

Located up on the Bench, Vineland Estates Winery made a splash in the Ontario wine world a few years ago, when its 1998 Meritage was priced at $125, an unprecedented price for a Canadian wine. It's still Canada's most expensive table wine on release, and it drew more attention to this winery, which had already earned a reputation as a leading producer of Riesling. Riesling, in fact, flows in Vineland Estates' corporate veins. It began as a 50-acre (20-hectare) Riesling vineyard planted in 1979 by German vine nurseryman and winemaker, Hermann Weis. His aim was to demonstrate that Riesling

VINELAND ESTATES WINERY

would perform well on the slopes of the Niagara Escarpment. Weis called his vineyard St. Urbanshof, after his vineyard and winery in the Mosel region, and once he was satisfied that his vines had taken, he established a winery.

Weis sold winery and vines in 1992 to businessman John Howard, and Vineland quickly won a reputation as one of the region's premier producers. Early on, it benefited from some good publicity. In 1993, Vineland's winemaker, Allan Schmidt (now the winery president) and his younger brother Brian (now the chief winemaker) dog-sledded to the magnetic North Pole and took 12 bottles of Vineland icewine with them, ostensibly for "polarized aging." (One of these bottles was added to each vintage of icewine in the following years.)

The $125 Meritage attracted attention, too. That pricing came about after Vineland's 1998 Meritage beat hundreds of Bordeaux blends from regions like Bordeaux and California, to win the silver medal at Vinexpo, France's most prestigious wine show. Allan Schmidt says he was called by a European journalist, who was amazed that a Canadian wine had done so well. "He asked me how much our '98 Meritage sold for, and I told him it hadn't been priced yet. 'Well', he said, 'the wine that got the gold medal sells for $150 to $200, depending where you buy it, and the wine that got the bronze medal sells for $50 to $70. So your silver medal wine must sell for $125'. And I said, 'Yeah, that's about what we're selling it for.'" The 1997 vintage, which had earlier been released at $60, was re-priced at $125, and that price has been applied to all subsequent vintages.

In the late 1990s, Ontario wine was still widely regarded as third-rate, and hardly worth $12, let alone ten times that. What's astonishing isn't just the $125 price tag of the 1998 Meritage, but the original $60 price of the 1997 vintage. Even now, there are few Ontario wines (except for icewines) that sell for more than $50.

The Schmidt brothers who now run Vineland Estates come from a deeply rooted wine family. Their grandfather operated a vineyard in British Columbia's Okanagan Valley, and their father was one of the founders of Sumac Ridge Estate Winery

there. Allan Schmidt worked as a winemaker at Sumac before coming to Vineland Estates in 1987, and he was joined by his brother, Brian, in 1991. Vineland now has 250 acres (100 hectares) of vineyards and produces up to 50,000 cases a year. Riesling is still the signature wine, but the Vineland portfolio also includes fine Pinot Blanc, Pinot Gris, and Bordeaux reds.

The Vineland property is one of Niagara's most popular destinations for wine-tourists. It has a cluster of stone buildings, including the original 1840s farmhouse and a carriage house that dates to 1857, which is now used for private functions. Vineland is a popular location for upscale weddings, and The Restaurant at Vineland Estates, which has a 4-Diamond award, is one of the most prestigious in Niagara.

Kacaba Vineyards

Kacaba Vineyards, also located off King Street on the Bench, is the brainchild of Michael Kacaba (pronounced Ka-SA-ba), a Toronto lawyer, who bought the land in 1997. Rob Warren, who was winemaker from 2001 to 2004, says the land, which used to graze horses, "was set for development and Mike Kacaba didn't want to see that happen, so he planted grapes, which is a pretty good thing. Once there are houses on land, there's not much you can do with it. The soil structure's so messed up you can never, ever have crops on it again."

Kacaba has 15 acres (six hectares) of vineyards that are planted with only four varieties, all red: Cabernet Sauvignon, Cabernet Franc, Merlot, and one of the region's first blocks of Syrah. The vines provide enough grapes for about two-thirds of their needs for red wines, so they source the rest, including Pinot Noir and Gamay. They buy all the grapes for their white wines, which are Chardonnay, Pinot Gris, and Riesling. As much as possible they source grapes from growers on the Bench "so as to make our wine as distinct as possible, wine with a Bench terroir."

From a couple of thousand cases of wine in 1999, using only purchased grapes, Kacaba hit its stride with 5,000 cases in 2002 when their own vines were mature. The aim is to take production to

10,000 cases. Rob Warren joined as winemaker in 2001 and made that vintage with legendary Niagara winemaker Jim Warren (who is no relation). On Rob Warren's watch, there was no Kacaba style. "We make the wines the way we like them to taste. We like them to be approachable when they're young, so you don't need to cellar them for years. That's not to say you can't age them, because it depends on the vintage. If you get a hot, hot year and good tannins, you can have good ageability."

Warren preferred working with red wines and especially liked making Syrah: "the vineyard looks after itself; it's pretty resistant to diseases." His Syrahs are in a Northern Rhône style, big and quite peppery, and in fact many vintages of Kacaba wine are distinguished by being big and mouth-filling but well structured as well. The reds get a lot of barrel time, with the reserve wines spending a year in new oak and several months more in used barrels.

Rob Warren left Kacaba in 2004 and his place was taken by Beth Mischuk, who had been assistant winemaker since 2002. In 2005, John Tummon, who has long experience as an award-winning amateur winemaker, came on board as Kacaba's winemaker. He says he plans to carry on Kacaba's emphasis on premium VQA wines, including full-bodied reds and Chardonnays, and is especially keen to work with the Syrah.

Featherstone Estate Winery & Vineyard

When you visit Featherstone Winery, you're greeted by a large piece of pink granite with a feather carved into it. It also features the name of the winery, but the feather and the stone make the point. The feather is a reference to the fact that the owners of the winery, David Johnson and Louise Engel, used to run the Guelph Poultry Gourmet Market. "If it had feathers, we sold it!" Louise says. As for the stone, it's a reference to the limestone of the Bench.

Back in Guelph, they used to buy a lot of white wine to make the gravy they sold to go with their chickens, and one day it struck Louise Engel that they might make their own wine. She said, "David, can't you make this? How hard can it be?" This led Johnson to amateur winemaking. He excelled

RETIRED BARRELS

at it, won prizes, and started to think of opening a winery. In 1998 he and Engel bought a 20-acre (eight-hectare) vineyard on the Beamsville Bench, built a winery, and began to make wine in 1999. In 2003, David Johnson was crowned Grape King, and Featherstone was named Winery of the Year, no paltry achievement, given that Featherstone had been in operation only four years.

The vineyard has a good range of varieties, including Riesling, Chardonnay, Gamay, Sauvignon Blanc, Pinot Noir, and Merlot. It stands out as one of the few vineyards in Niagara that are cultivated without the use of insecticides. One reason for this is that Johnson and Engel live in an 1830s wood-frame farmhouse on the property, so they would have to breathe any insecticides they applied.

Featherstone isn't an organic vineyard, but they aim to reduce chemical use to the bare minimum. Instead, they rely on natural predators and remedies to take care of pests. They release lady-bugs and lacewings to take care of aphids, and also spray with a mixture of shark oil and garlic. It makes the place smell like bouillabaisse, Engel says, but it keeps insects down and seems to invigorate the vines. More impressively, they unleash a hawk on birds. Amadeus is a Harris hawk, a species native to Central America, and he's been trained by Louise Engel, who obtained her falconer licence in 2005. Amadeus deals definitively with a few birds a week, and frightens many more away from the vines.

Featherstone produces a limited range of high-quality wines. The three Chardonnays include one aged in French and one aged in Canadian oak barrels. The wines can be rich and complex, and there's a nice contrast between the different oaks. As for reds, the most popular is a Baco Noir-Cabernet

Franc blend, and they give an intriguing twist to Cabernet Franc by aging it in cherrywood barrels. Featherstone's best-known wine, though, is Gamay, which has proved to be a surprising success. The 2002 vintage won a gold medal at the Ontario Wine Awards and the 2004 won Best of Class at the All-Canadian Wine Awards. (The 2003 wasn't entered for any awards because only a small volume was made.) With these medals, demand for the Gamay took flight as smoothly as Amadeus.

Stoney Ridge Estate Winery

Stoney Ridge Estate Winery has one of Niagara's longer lineages, which means it goes back more than ten years. Its predecessor, Stoney Ridge Cellars, was founded at Wylie's Farm in Stoney Creek in 1985. That year, prize-winning amateur winemaker Jim Warren and two partners made 500 cases of an impressive 11 different wines. Four years later,

VINES IN SPRING

production zoomed to 4,000 cases and the business seemed on the upswing.

When the North American Free Trade Agreement seemed to doom the Ontario wine industry to die under a tsunami of California wine, the provincial government offered growers cash to pull out their grapes. Jim Warren's partners took the offer and eventually planted the vineyard in Christmas trees. Warren then partnered with Murray Puddicombe, now owner of Puddicombe Farms Winery, and the two opened a new facility in Winona to produce much larger volumes. By 1997, production had reached 27,000 cases, and the portfolio included an astonishing 60 different products, including un-oaked Chardonnay, Pinot Noir, Riesling, and some fruit wines.

The Puddicombe-Warren partnership ended that year, and Jim Warren, who by then was already achieving legendary winemaker status in the region (he was named Winemaker of the Year in 1997), relocated Stoney Ridge to Vineland. Two years later, the peripatetic Warren left Stoney Ridge and his assistant, Liubomir Popovici, took over. Popovici had been chief winemaker at one of Romania's largest wine producers from 1995 to 1999 and did a stint in Finland, making fruit wines. He arrived in Canada early in 1999, and Jim Warren hired him for Stoney Ridge right away.

By the early 2000s, Stoney Ridge was making about 40,000 cases of wine a year, making it one of the bigger medium-sized wineries in the region, and in 2002 the winery adopted its current name and began to refocus on quality wine production. Throughout this meandering history, more complicated than most in Niagara, Jim Warren was the constant thread. Even though he'd left the company, he returned as a consultant in 2002 to start making an annual Founder's Signature Collection of wines.

Stoney Ridge also has a Wine Library, but unlike most libraries, which are reserves of older vintages for winery use, this one sells to the public. The library is the result of one of those serendipitous events. When the winery moved to its present location in 1998, thousands of bottles of older vintages were mistakenly stored in the basement of an unused house on one of the Stoney Ridge vineyards. They included a hundred different limited edition wines going back to 1985, all made by Jim Warren and all of which turned out to be in excellent condition. The Wine Library opened in 2002 to sell these wines (and other older vintages as they're released), and it offers a rare opportunity for people to see how Niagara wines can age.

All three Stoney Ridge vineyards are located on the Beamsville Bench. There's the small, three-acre (one hectare) McGrade Vineyard, planted in Pinot Noir and located close to the winery so, they say, they can keep an eye on that notoriously fickle variety. Then there's the 40-acre (16-hectare) Cuesta Vineyard, with Pinot Noir, Cabernet Franc, Cabernet Sauvignon, and Merlot. The last in the trio is the 70-acre (28-hectare) Kew Vineyard in Beamsville, where Stoney Ridge sources many varieties, including Chenin Blanc, Gewürztraminer, Riesling, Sauvignon Blanc, Baco Noir, and Zweigelt. The average age of these vines is about 30 years.

Stoney Ridge has a big portfolio, making many different varieties in different styles, but their best include Chardonnays, Cabernet Franc, and Pinot Noir. There are a couple of gaps, like a varietal Cabernet Sauvignon, because they haven't been able to locate fruit they consider good enough. What they grow, they incorporate into their Bordeaux blends.

Popovici has particular styles in mind as he makes the wine. He likes his whites to be "clean and fruity," and he introduced Pinot Gris in 2002. He also likes fruity reds and finds his Merlot to be consistently good, but he's a true believer in Cabernet Franc. Gamay can also be very good, Popovici says, but "consumers aren't as attracted to Cabernets." As for Baco Noir, it's great in Ontario, "and in terms of price to quality, it's just great for the consumer." He also likes making Pinot Noir and, like most winemakers, finds it "very challenging, and you don't have the chance to enhance it by blending." Among Stoney Ridge's successful dessert wines, late-harvests and a port-style fortified wine stand out.

JORDAN

Flat Rock Cellars

Flat Rock Cellars, officially opened in the spring of 2005, has one of the more interesting designs in Niagara. Located at the top of the Jordan Bench, and built into the side of a ridge, it's a hexagonal

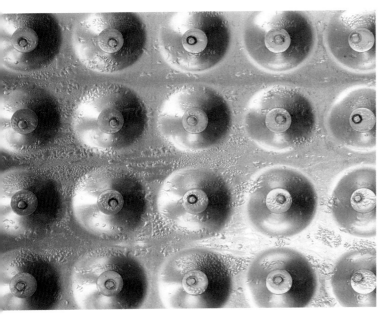

CONDENSATION FROM COOLED WINE

building. When you view it mirrored in the pond on the property, it's reminiscent of a pagoda. Inside, it's all open-concept, with the press, tanks, and barrels organized on five levels to make maximum use of gravity when moving wine from one stage of production to the next. The retail store and tasting area, which are attached to the winery, command a stunning view over Lake Ontario.

Owner Ed Madronich explains the name: while they were digging the trenches for the under-drainage of the vineyard, all they pulled up were flat rocks. The drainage forces the vines to push their roots deeper into the soil, and adds complexity to flavours, and so Flat Rock, Madronich says, "refers to the land upon which the vineyard is planted, along with our commitment to low yields and quality grape production." Just in case visitors wonder

about the name, a stack of the rocks, looking a bit like an Inuit Inukshuk, greets you at the winery entrance.

Flat Rock is a 98-acre (39-hectare) property with 80 acres (32 hectares) of vines. All of its wines are made from estate-grown grapes, except for icewine, which is made from purchased Vidal. The growing regime is designed to maximize quality, with green-harvesting removing up to half the bunches. The grapes are hand picked and collected in small, 20-kilogram baskets, rather than large bins in which the grapes on the bottom can be prematurely crushed by the weight of those above.

The winery embodies many environmentally-sensitive features. It's heated and cooled from the artificial pond next to the winery, and is estimated to use only 20 to 25 percent of the energy of a normal facility its size. An ozone machine, rather than chemicals, is used to clean the barrels and tanks, and waste water is filtered by natural biological means. Outside, they've planted trees to reduce evaporation and installed a windmill to aerate the pond. Flat Rock has innovated in other ways, too, and places a premium on preserving their wines' freshness. When they take barrel samples, staff quickly drop dry ice through the bung-hole so as to minimize the wine's exposure to oxygen.

Once they're bottled, all Flat Rock wines are sealed with screw cap, rather than cork or artificial cork-shaped stoppers. While a few Niagara wineries use screw caps for some of their wines (usually the whites and especially for lower-end whites), no winery until Flat Rock took the plunge to go all the way. As a new winery, they had the luxury of deciding what kind of bottling and closure they wanted, unlike established wineries that have to invest in new bottling lines to convert to screw cap. Even so, despite the general trend toward screw caps, Niagara's newest wineries have generally opted for natural corks or artificial equivalents for most of their wines.

Flat Rock's first winemaker was Darryl Brooker, an Australian who had worked in the Barossa Valley and New Zealand. He made Flat Rock's first vintages in 2003 and 2004, but left in 2005 to make wine at Hillebrand Estates. Brooker's Flat Rock

wines are characterized by real fruit purity and varietal authenticity. They include an aromatic, crisp vineyard-designated Riesling (Nadja's Vineyard, named for Madronich's wife), and an elegant 2004 Chardonnay. There's also a wine called "Twisted," an off-dry, aromatic white made of Gewürztraminer and Riesling with a dash of Chardonnay. Pinot Noir is slated to become a star in Flat Rock's line-up. The 2003 vintage produced a wine with complex, intense, and juicy fruit character and gripping tannins. It's what a lot of people think of as Burgundian in style, and that goes along with Brooker's intentions. Off the Burgundy track, though, there's also an elegant Pinot Noir Rosé. It has a stunning bronze-salmon colour, and has a lot more complexity than you often find in a rosé.

Cave Spring Cellars

If you're looking for a destination winery in this area, Cave Spring Cellars is probably the one.

It's located in Jordan village, which was founded in the 19th century to provide services for local farmers. On pretty, treelined Main Street, Cave Spring runs not only the winery but also a well-known restaurant (On the Twenty) and a boutique hotel (The Twenty Inn). The winery and restaurant are located in what used to be the massive (80,000 square foot) Jordan Wines facility, along with other stores that sell antiques and clothing. And you can buy wine, of course, from Cave Spring's retail store. There you find a fine range of whites, reds, and dessert wines, with an emphasis on whites and, within that, on Riesling. Cave Spring has staked out a formidable reputation as a Riesling producer, and its dry and off-dry styles are bestsellers.

This is one of Niagara's more established wineries, established by Len Pennachetti and Angelo Pavan in 1986. Pennachetti's earliest exposure to wine was in his grandfather's labrusca vineyard. Giuseppe Pennachetti came to Niagara in the 1920s to work on the Welland Canal, and planted a vineyard when he retired. Len Pennachetti became interested through one of his high school teachers, who just happened to be doing a graduate degree on the suitability of Niagara for vinifera varieties. This was about 1970, when few growers were planting vinifera, and the dominant view was still that the vines wouldn't survive the region's winters.

Len Pennachetti became convinced of the viability of vinifera, and a few years later he and his father chartered a small plane to fly them over the region to identify promising areas. They decided that the area on the Beamsville Bench occupied by Cave Spring Farm looked ideal and bought the land. The Pennachettis planted a vineyard there in 1978 and began selling the fruit to wineries. This was only a side-interest, because Len had started a doctorate in philosophy and was heading for an academic career. That ended when his father died in 1985. He left his studies to help deal with his father's estate, and soon after was approached by Thomas Muckle, a Hamilton physician and accomplished amateur winemaker. Pennachetti tasted some of Muckle's Rieslings and was impressed enough to go along with his proposal that they start a winery. He jokes that he swapped "Vico for vino," a reference to the 18th-century Italian philosopher Giambattista Vico.

The first vintages were made at the Hillebrand winery, but they soon needed extra room and leased space in the Jordan Wines building. Muckle and Pennachetti also took on a new partner, Angelo Pavan, who was also doing a Ph.D. in philosophy. Pavan had no experience as a winemaker, but took wine appreciation and technical courses and soon took over winemaking. Muckle later left the partnership to start Thirty Bench winery, where he still makes the Rieslings.

When the Jordan Wines building went up for sale in 1989, Pennachetti and Pavan thought about buying it, but were daunted by its 80,000 square feet. It was Pennachetti's wife, Helen Young, who saw the possibilities of using some of the space for a restaurant and retail stores. This was forward thinking. No Niagara winery had its own restaurant at that time, and when On the Twenty opened in 1993, it was the first winery restaurant in Ontario. It's named for Twenty Mile Creek, which runs behind the winery.

Cave Spring draws fruit from vineyards on the Bench that are owned by Len Pennachetti and his younger brother, Tom. Together they own 200 acres (80 hectares) of vines, about half in Riesling. Their other varieties include Chardonnay, Pinot Noir, Gamay, and Cabernet Franc. Cave Spring's vines are planted more densely than most in Niagara. This forces the vines to compete with one another for water and nutrients, and they drive their roots deep into the clay and loam of the Bench.

They buy about 30 percent of the grapes they need to produce their annual 50,000 cases. Some of their wines come from several districts in Niagara. The 2004 dry Riesling, for example, draws mostly on grapes from the Bench and the rest from the Creek Shores sub-appellation on Lake Ontario. Tom Pennachetti points out that "with Riesling, we're going after heavy clay soils. The style of Riesling we make doesn't come from every soil type." Riesling accounts for just over half of Cave Spring's total production, and they produce several styles, dry and off-dry. All Cave Spring Rieslings achieve a fine degree of balance between fruit and acidity and have a characteristic mineral note. For Pavan, Riesling is the grape Niagara does best. Not only do Niagara wineries like Cave Spring produce elegant expressions of it, but Riesling is among the hardier vines, an important consideration in light of recent winters that have killed or damaged more sensitive varieties like Merlot and Sauvignon Blanc.

But Cave Spring is no one-wine wonder. It makes several notable Chardonnays, generally in a restrained, structured Old World style with careful barrel aging and a delightful wine from the Chardonnay Musqué clone, which produces a wine reminiscent of a Gewürztraminer in style, with soft spicy notes. In 2002, Cave Spring also made a very successful Chenin Blanc.

Red wines make up a quarter of the Cave Spring list, and there are fairly full-bodied numbers from Bordeaux varieties plus a very good single-vineyard Syrah. The Pinot Noir has good fruit and food-friendly acidity, but it's Gamay that Cave Spring makes exceptionally well, with quite rich and complex cherry flavours and spicy notes. Tom Pennachetti laments the fact that Gamay hasn't caught on among wine drinkers. It's a popular entry-level wine, he says, "and at the high end, it's made some of the best red wines in Niagara. At the high end it can be one of the most expressive red wines."

There's also a sparkling wine, made in the traditional method, with a second fermentation in the bottle. Curiously, it's made from Chardonnay and Pinot Noir (two of the Champagne grapes) rather than from Riesling, like most quality German Sekt sparkling wines. But for the dessert wines, we're back to Riesling again. There are icewines, of course, but the most popular Cave Spring dessert wine is Indian Summer, a late-harvest Riesling that, year after year, offers beautiful pungent stone-fruit flavours. It's Angelo Pavan's favourite among the wines he makes. The grapes are picked after the first freeze of the winter, and he loves the way the Riesling comes through, with rich fruit on a clean acid spine. "You don't get this with botrytis-affected wines," he says. "The botrytis can smother the fruit, but with this one you can tell you're drinking Riesling."

Harbour Estates Winery

Fruit of a different kind is in the lineage of Harbour Estates Winery. In 1913, Fraser Mowat's grandfather arrived in Niagara from Scotland and planted a peach orchard. Fraser's father also grew peaches. When Fraser and his wife, Darlene, bought land on the Jordan Harbour, an inlet of Lake Ontario, in 1979, they planted . . . peaches.

But in the early '90s, "when the peach market was very soft, no pun intended," Mowat looked for new opportunities and found himself working for Farm Credit Canada, which lent money to farmers. "That was about '96–'97, when the wine industry was really starting to break loose, and I started chasing wineries to lend money to. At

VINES IN WINTER

the same time, the wineries were starting to look at the amount of grapes planted in the Peninsula and say, 'Hey, we need whites, we need reds, we need viniferas.'" Mowat was involved in the financial side of the industry but started to think about growing grapes on his property. In 1997 he had an acre (0.4 hectares) ready for replanting with peach trees, but he planted Merlot instead. The next year, three more acres (one hectare) were ready for new peach trees, but instead he planted more Merlot and some Cabernet Sauvignon.

The Mowats realized they had a unique property for a winery, and by late 1998 Fraser Mowat had decided to build one. "My wife keeps reminding me it was my decision!" In spring 1999 they ripped out all the peach trees and planted Cabernet Sauvignon, Cabernet Franc, and Merlot and now have 30 acres (12 hectares) in vines.

TRIMMING THE VINES ON A HOT SUMMER DAY

John Howard, the owner of Vineland Estate, assisted and advised at the start, taking the view that there was room for all kinds of new wineries in Niagara, as long as they were making top-notch wines. "He was even willing to put his winemaker where his mouth was to make sure our first vintage was a decent one" and provided Vineland's winemaker, Brian Schmidt, to consult on the 1999 vintage, Harbour Estates' first. Another Vineland winemaker, Jeff Innes, moved to Harbour Estates in November 2000 and finished the winemaking that Fraser Mowat and his son, Ken, had started. When Innes left in 2002, Ken Mowat stepped into the cellar, just in time to make the big 2002 vintage. From 3,500 cases in 2001, Harbour Estates made 10,000 in 2002. Mowat admits he was apprehensive. Ken,

who was only 22 at the time, had made some wine before, but 100 litres, not 100,000. His first wine, a 2002 dry Riesling, won several medals, as did other wines from that vintage. He continues to be Harbour Estates' winemaker, cementing its identity as a family winery.

Fraser and Darlene Mowat see Harbour Estates as having two characteristics. First, it's tied to their location: "It's a very beautiful property, with 1,800 feet of frontage on Jordan Harbour and surrounded by Carolinian forest. We used to walk through the property and say, 'This is just beautiful. It's too bad the general public can't see it or get closer to it.'" It's now open to the public and offers walking tours through the vineyards to the shoreline, as well as many events from spring to fall.

The wines are accessible, too. Harbour Estates' style is easy-drinking and smooth and designed for "people who drink wine, don't necessarily know a lot about wine, but certainly know what they like, maybe can't describe it, don't know any of the lingo." They include three that play on the winery's water-side location: Harbour Estates Sunrise (Vidal and Chardonnay), Sunset (a rosé made of Riesling and Merlot), and Midnight (Cabernet Franc, Cabernet Sauvignon, and Merlot). The winery's Baco Noir, initially made as an entry-level wine, proved to be a runaway success. It has good concentrated fruit with spicy, smoky notes. The flagship wine, called Premier Vintage, is made of five Bordeaux varieties and is produced only in selected vintages. There are also dessert wines (late-harvest and a range of white and red icewines) and a few fruit wines. Curiously, none is made from peaches. They've tried, Fraser Mowat says, but have never been happy with the results.

Thirteenth Street Winery

Not far away is one of Niagara's cult wineries. Thirteenth Street Winery is housed in a utilitarian building in the midst of the estate vineyard. On official release days the parking lot overflows with cars from Niagara, Toronto, and farther afield as the winery's fans make sure they get their allotment of the new releases, some of which are limited to two bottles per customer. It's not surprising that much of Thirteenth Street Winery's 1,500 case production quickly disappears, hauled off by a stream of cars heading down Thirteenth Street.

The tasting room is open only on Saturdays and Sundays, reflecting the fact that the winemakers generally work here only on weekends. Thirteenth Street is a partnership of four men who have other jobs during the week: Gunther Funk is a hydro-geologist, Ken Douglas a lawyer, Erv Willms a chemical engineer, and Herb Jacobson a hydraulic engineer. They were all keen amateur winemakers who got together regularly, and in 1997 they started thinking about opening a winery. The following year, they obtained a licence. They share the wine-making facility, where they make wine from Funk's G.H. Funk vineyard at the winery location and Erv Willms' Sandstone vineyard in Niagara-on-the-Lake. The two vineyards produce different grapes. The Funk vineyard is cooler and is mainly planted

with Riesling, Pinot Noir, and Sauvignon Blanc, while Willms has planted mainly Gamay, as well as Chardonnay and the red Bordeaux varieties in his warmer location.

Gunther Funk's apprenticeship in viticulture and winemaking was a blend of smart decisions and trial and error. When he and his wife, Mary, bought a vineyard in 1983, they had no farming experience. This could have been considered a disadvantage to successful grape-growing, but Funk puts a positive spin on it. He says that he had "no preconceived ideas about growing grapes," so he was open to the new techniques being used in Australia, California and parts of Europe. He was among the first in Niagara to appreciate the importance of canopy management and crop-thinning.

Some experiments didn't work. The Funks decided to plant some varieties because they were what they liked to drink, not because they promised to grow well in Niagara. Zinfandel and Petite Sirah came and went, as did Nebbiolo and Syrah after ten years. Despite reducing yields dramatically, they weren't happy with the wines.

Initially, the Funks sold their grapes to Jordan Wines in St. Catharines. Their crop was quite small, and they once won a prize for supplying the smallest lot of grapes among the growers who supplied Jordan. On that occasion, Funk recalls, they had delivered a third of a ton of grapes in the back of their 1983 Chevy station wagon. In 1987, after Jordan Wines closed, Funk sold his grapes to Hillebrand and once again he was unhappy to see his low-cropped, hand-harvested grapes go into the same hopper as high-yield, machine-harvested grapes from other growers. He started selling his high-quality juice to amateur winemakers like him-self, although he occasionally sold to wineries.

As testament to the quality of Funk's grapes, his Pinot Noir fruit was used for the first Three Guys collection of Pinot Noirs in the mid-1990s. Three of Niagara's leading winemakers—Jim Warren (Stoney Ridge Estate), John Marynissen (Marynissen Estate), and Eddy Gurinskas (Lakeview Cellars)—had been in an amateur winemakers' club before becoming profes-sionals. In the Three Guys collection, each makes Pinot

Noir from grapes from the same vineyard, so as to show the different imprint each puts on the same fruit. (A fourth bottle in the set is a blend of the three.)

Erv Willms, Funk's fellow vineyard owner at Thirteenth Street, followed a different trajectory into wine. He and his wife, Esther, bought a run-down vineyard in Niagara-on-the-Lake in 1981. Willms had grown up in a fruit-farming family and didn't like the idea of growing fruit that had to be harvested all summer, so he decided to replant in vines. Paul Bosc, who had just opened Château des Charmes and was gung-ho about vinifera, urged Willms to plant those varieties, and he did: Gamay, Riesling, and Chardonnay. For the first few years he sold the fruit to Bosc. He bought more land in 1992 (to total 18 acres, or seven hectares) and added Cabernet Franc and Cabernet Sauvignon to his repertoire of vines.

NETTED GRAPES

His vineyard is called Sandstone after all the stones, rocks, and even boulders in the soil. "We have put boulders to good use as a 'rock garden' in our front yard," Willms notes. With the opening of Thirteenth Street, Willm began to reduce his yields (from five down to two or three tonnes an acre), cut the use of fertilizer and sprays, eliminate herbicides, and manage the vines' canopies more rigorously.

Willms' and Funk's partners in Thirteenth Street Winery share their commitment to producing high-quality grapes and wine. They prefer to call themselves winegrowers; they harvest and sort all their grapes by hand and ferment the juice in small lots. And they strongly believe in fair pricing for their wines, even though there's enough demand to allow them to raise their prices. They're proud of the good value they offer.

The results are impressive across the board. The Funk vineyard produces two very good and

remarkably inexpensive wines (a rosé and a Riesling), as well as an impressive Meritage. Under the Sandstone label there are finely structured Chardonnays and two Gamays (one entry-level and one reserve) that rank among the variety's best expressions in Ontario, where Gamay is building a solid reputation.

Thirteenth Street is rightly proud of its sparkling wines, too. Gunther Funk says they have really worked to master the winemaking, and it's still very labour- and capital-intensive. "It also has the highest risk, because we're literally making wine we can't assess for three or more years. Right now, we feel we're consistent and are producing some of Canada's best." Then there's Erv's Burger Blend, which combines 60 percent Cabernet Franc along with Cabernet Sauvignon, Gamay, and Merlot. It has slightly funky aromas, dark fruit flavours with spicy, pepper notes, and nice tannins. And it shows that for all Thirteenth Street's commitment to rigorous grape growing and winemaking, they're adventurous, too.

As for the future, the Thirteenth Street four are looking at various other red blends, and hope to produce a Bordeaux white blend. (A few years ago they produced a wine called Musgari, a blend of Muscat, Riesling, and Gewürztraminer, but discontinued it when they pulled the Gewürztraminer out.) This is one winery to watch.

Creekside Estate Winery

Creekside Estate Winery is located at the crest of a hill as Fourth Avenue follows its undulating route through vineyards and orchards. Formerly V. P. Cellars, it was bought in 1998 by Peter Jensen, whose background is in the brewing industry and home-winemaking stores, and Laura McCain-Jensen, of the New Brunswick-based McCain Foods. Their attention turned to wine after they honeymooned in California wine country. They've turned the languishing V. P. Cellars into a winery that consistently produces high-quality wines.

The first vintage was 1998, but they bought grapes that year because the vines in their newly acquired vineyards had been neglected and weren't fit for harvesting. Instead, Charles Pillitteri,

of Pillitteri Estates, sold them some Pinot Noir and Sauvignon Blanc, varieties that were just starting to make an impression in the region. Ann Sperling came on board as consulting winemaker, and made wines that were so impressive they created an instant buzz about Creekside.

ROLLED UP WIRE FENCING AFTER FALL HARVEST

Creekside's first full-time winemaker was Australian Marcus Ansems. He had extensive experience making wine in Australia, New Zealand, Oregon, and Ontario and was given the task of transforming the winery and vineyards. He started by developing the 18-acre (seven-hectare) vineyard at the winery where he planted Cabernet Sauvignon, Sauvignon Blanc, and Shiraz. Ansems' Australian roots showed in his commitment to Shiraz at a time when it was just beginning to spark some interest in Niagara. It proved a sound decision. Not only has it been contributing some impressive wines, but the Shiraz vines have coped better with very cold winters than Cabernet Sauvignon and Merlot. A second vineyard (50 acres/20 hectares) near St. David's contributes more Shiraz and Cabernet Sauvignon, along with Chardonnay, Viognier, Merlot, and Pinot

VINE IN WINTER

Noir. Creekside buys the rest of the grapes it needs for its 25,000 cases from independent growers.

Ansems also developed the winemaking facilities in 1999 and the following year oversaw the construction of an underground aging cellar that holds up to 600 barrels. His wines, especially Sauvignon Blanc, Syrah, and a Cabernet Sauvignon-Cabernet Franc-Merlot blend called Laura's Blend, reinforced Creekside's reputation. He left for Australia and then British Columbia in 2002. His place was taken by Craig McDonald, an Australian who had been assistant winemaker, and Rob Power, a former sommelier from Peterborough, Ontario, and graduate of Brock University's viticulture and oenology program. More recently another Brock graduate, Geoff Taylor, joined the team.

McDonald and Power are a formidable duo, turning out an almost faultless range of wines. Highlights include Pinot Grigio and Pinot Gris, which are made in different styles. McDonald says they spend more time on the Pinot Gris vines than any another variety except for Pinot Noir, and it shows. The attention to the vineyards has also shown them the different flavour profiles that various sites give Sauvignon Blanc.

Creekside's reserve Pinot Noirs, from 10- to 14-year-old vines, can offer rich, lush fruit. They are, McDonald says, "as full-on a Pinot Noir as you'd get in New Zealand," which has developed a reputation for that variety. The Shirazes are remarkably intense, even in some cooler years, and have stylish peppery notes. The other reds are also very well made, delivering good complex fruit qualities and excellent balance.

Creekside is a dynamic winery that continues to evolve. They've added to their attraction as a destination by building the Wine Deck and Grill to serve lunches during the summer. Each menu item is accompanied by a recommended wine from the Creekside range. The barrel cellar is also used for private functions and full-scale meals.

In 2004, Peter Jensen and Laura McCain-Jensen formed Canadian Wine Partners with Barry Katzman, former president of Stoney Ridge Cellars. Their company will form partnerships with strong regional wineries to benefit from common operations while maintaining their own identity. The group currently owns Creekside and Blomidon Ridge Winery (formerly Habitant) in Nova Scotia's Annapolis Valley.

The first major initiative of Canadian Wine Partners was a joint venture of Jensen and McCain-Jensen with Canadian pro golfer Mike Weir in the Mike Weir Estate Winery. The Weir vineyard is a 51-acre (20-hectare) site planted in 1999, with the first wines released in May 2005—a 2001 Chardonnay and a 2002 Cabernet-Merlot—both made at Creekside. The proceeds from wine sales go to the Mike Weir Foundation, which benefits children's charities. A hospitality and retail centre and Mike Weir gallery, with an elevated perch overlooking the vineyards, opens in Niagara-on-the-Lake in 2006.

Le Clos Jordanne

One more winery will soon appear on the Jordan landscape: Le Clos Jordanne, which is a joint pro-ject of Vincor and the big Burgundy-based wine company Boisset. Its aim is to produce mainly Pinot Noir and Chardonnay, not only vinified in a Burgundian style, but envisaged like Burgundy, from vineyard to bottle, as specific to the land in which the vines grow. Some of the wines will be labelled by the names of the vineyards, like Premier Cru Burgundies. Le Clos Jordanne has four vineyards, totalling 130 acres (52 hectares), three on what winemaker Thomas Bachelder calls "the sweet spot" of the Bench and another above Flat Rock Cellars.

Farming is organic, with some biodynamic influences. Bachelder says that the essence "isn't to artificially correct the vineyards to a magic number. The idea is, without letting the plants suffer any deficiencies, to let them evolve." In this way, he says,

each vineyard will express itself through the grapes and each will make distinctive wine. He's enthusiastic about making Burgundy-style wine here because the soil gives a minerality he finds lacking in many New World Pinot Noirs and Chardonnays. Québec-born Bachelder trained and worked in Burgundy and Oregon (another Pinot Noir region) before coming to Niagara. His assistant, Isabelle Meunier, is also from Québec and Burgundy, but worked with Pinot Noir in New Zealand.

What excited Ontario's wine world about Le Clos Jordanne isn't just the partnership with a major Burgundy producer and the plan to transplant a little bit of Burgundy in Niagara, it's also that the winery building has been designed by iconic architect Frank Gehry, the Canadian who designed structures like the Guggenheim Museum in Bilbao, Spain. It will be unlike any other winery in Canada, with a high, undulating roofline that evokes clouds and hills. But what Gehry has referred to as a "cathedral of wine" is a way off yet. It was originally scheduled for completion in 2008, but the whole project has been delayed by severe winters that threw out the wine production schedule. Current plans are to break ground for the new building in 2007 or 2008, with completion two years later. Given the imaginative scale underlying Le Clos Jordanne, another couple of years seems negligible.

THE WINERIES OF ST. CATHARINES

Rockway Glen Golf Course and Estate Winery

In an age where Canadian, Australian, and South African professional golfers' names are appearing on wine labels, it's intriguing to find an actual golf course that makes its own wine. Slice your drive badly at the Rockway Glen Golf Course and Estate Winery and you might be looking for your ball among Chardonnay or Riesling vines.

The 18-hole Rockway Glen Golf Course, which is open to the public, is located between the Niagara Escarpment and the Rockway Conservation Area. It sits on land originally planted in vines that were pulled out as part of the vine-pull scheme following the 1989 Free Trade Agreement. Fairways and greens were planted in their place. In the late 1990s, a small vineyard was planted bordering the golf course, and there have been more plantings since 2002.

The winery opened in 2001, and the winemaker is Jeff Innes, who used to make Harbour Estates wines. The winery's current production is 4,000 cases a year, and the range includes Riesling, Chardonnay, Vidal, Gamay, Baco Noir, Cabernet-Merlot, and Cabernet Franc, along with late-harvest and ice-wine Vidals. They're on sale to the public in the retail store, and you can taste them with a meal in the club-house restaurant.

Under the retail store is a small wine museum. Its name, "Le Musée du Vin," might seem un petit peu pretentious, but in fact the artifacts on display—mainly viticultural implements from the 19th century—come from major wine regions in France: Alsace, Champagne, Burgundy, and Bordeaux.

Hernder Estate Winery

Farther along, Hernder Estate produces both grape and fruit wines from a winery opened in 1993. It's housed in a post-and-beam four-storey barn that dates back to 1867, and this heritage building and Niagara's only covered bridge have made Hernder a popular location for many kinds of events, especially weddings. Hernder bills itself as Niagara's number one wedding winery, with couples coming from all over the world to be married.

The winery is only one part of the Hernder business. Fred Hernder runs one of Ontario's biggest independent grape-growing operations, with seven farms comprising 500 acres (200 hectares) of vines—about the same area of vineyards as the entire Prince Edward County wine region. They produce grapes that are variously used for juice and jams (the Concord variety in particular), and wine kits for people to make wine at home or in establishments where customers can make their own wine.

The best grapes, though, are reserved for Hernder Estate wines. The winery produces about 30,000 cases a year in a sometimes bewildering range. It includes a number of vinifera varietals like Riesling, Chardonnay, Gewürztraminer, Chenin Blanc, Chardonnay Musqué, Cabernet Franc, Merlot, Cabernet Sauvignon, and hybrids and crosses such as Vidal, Chambourcin, Morio Muscat, Baco Noir and Maréchal Foch. There are also dessert wines: late-harvest, select late-harvest, and both red and white icewines.

Winemaker Ray Cornell, a native of the Niagara region, worked at other area wineries before becoming Hernder's founding winemaker. He especially likes working with Riesling, and it shows in the often elegant examples he makes year after year. They're crisp with good fruit expression and have won wide critical praise. Cornell is no slouch with the reds, either. His 1999 Unfiltered Cabernet Franc is a big, brooding number, with rich, dark fruit and ripe tannins. It won Best Canadian Cabernet Franc and

Best Value Canadian Red Wine at the 2002 Canadian Wine Awards. That's another thing: Hernder wines tend to be well priced for their quality.

Harvest Estate Wines

Harvest Estate Wines, located in St. Catharines not far from a shopping mall, is a sibling winery of Hernder Estates. It was established in 1999 and its wines are from a 10-acre (four-hectare) vineyard that was replanted with vinifera in 2002. Ray Cornell makes Harvest Estate's wines, too. The retail store and tasting room are a kilometre away from the vines and winery, and are strategically located in the Harvest Barn, which sells fresh produce and baked goods, enabling shoppers to buy wine and food in the same place. It goes under the slogan "All good things under one roof." In addition to a dozen fruit wines, Harvest Estate makes about 20 wines from vinifera and hybrid varieties, all VQA-certified, and all at affordable prices.

Henry of Pelham Family Estate Winery

If Harvest Estate's store was strategically located near St. Catharines, another winery is finding that St. Catharines is spreading towards it. But Henry of Pelham Family Estate Winery successfully retains its rural feel. With its distinctive blue labels that populate the Ontario VQA shelves of the LCBO, Henry of Pelham is one of Ontario's most successful wineries. It's also one of the longer established, but its beginnings were inauspicious.

In 1982, Paul Speck Sr., a Toronto schoolteacher, bought a piece of land that had earlier belonged to his great-great-grandfather, Henry Smith. Henry's father, Nicholas, had been granted the land in 1794 for helping the British during the American War of Independence. Subsequently, each of Nicholas' children (Henry was one of 14) was granted land

BARRELS PUT OUT TO PASTURE

in Niagara. Henry built an inn, in what was then the township of Pelham, and collected tolls along Pelham Road. He signed one document "Henry of Pelham." When Henry Smith died in 1856, he left the inn to an associate, and the land was divided up. The family and some of the land were reunited

WASHING THE CONTAINERS BEFORE HAND PICKING

when Paul Speck Sr. bought it in 1982, and in the following year Speck acquired more of the land as well as the building that had been Henry Smith's inn.

There might have been some nostalgia driving Speck's decision to opt for land that had belonged to earlier generations of his family, but he was equally driven by his aspiration to make wine. This was in the early days of the modern Ontario wine industry and if quality was starting to rise, it was doing so on a very gentle curve. But grape growers were planting more and more vinifera varieties, and Speck believed that a good winery had a future. He enlisted the labour of his three young sons, Paul Jr., Matthew, and Daniel—Paul, the eldest, was only 17 in 1984—and together they ripped out many of the Concord and Niagara varieties that were growing on their new property. They recontoured much of the land, put in

drainage, and shovel-planted Chardonnay, Riesling, and Baco Noir. Their first vintage was 1988.

The winery came on stream just as economic uncertainty began to swirl through the Peninsula. The free trade agreement with the United States raised the spectre of a tsunami of cheap California wine washing into Ontario and wiping out the fledgling quality wine industry. As the Specks were planting their vineyard, many others were being ripped out. But the Speck brothers also faced another, more personal, crisis. Their father was diagnosed with cancer and, from 1989 until his death in 1993, was unable to run the winery alone. Paul Jr. put his university studies on hold to work in the family business and brought on board Ron Giesbrecht, who had been making wine at Brights winery.

It was the beginning of a beautiful partnership. Business often blends with family and friendship as well as oil with water, but the three Speck brothers and Giesbrecht have been a successful team for more than 15 years. Paul Jr. is president of the winery, Matthew manages the vineyards, and Daniel looks after the healthy sales of the wines that Ron makes.

Henry of Pelham's administrative offices and retail store are housed in the restored inn, while a restaurant, located in a coach house, serves meals during the tourist season. The site is surrounded by the 150 acres (60 hectares) of vineyards (in the summer evenings there are performances of Shakespeare among the vines) that provide about two-thirds of the grapes the winery uses each year. The rest are bought from growers in the Beamsville Bench and Niagara-on-the-Lake districts.

The winemaking facilities are housed in a large building that has all the elegance of an aircraft hangar. It's not one of those iconic designer facilities that have sprung up on the Niagara landscape in the last few years, but it produces excellent wine. Daniel Speck says of the winery and warehouse, "They're not pretty, but they work. They're like the family. We're not pretty, but we work."

There's no doubt that the whole operation works. Henry of Pelham has become one of the most successful wineries in the region, with a good range of whites, reds, and other styles. Although production is almost evenly split between white and red wine, the winery has developed a reputation for reds in particular. They've been especially successful with Baco Noir, a hybrid, which is ironic given that the modern Niagara wine industry was founded on the switch from hybrid to vinifera varieties. But Henry of Pelham's entry-level Baco Noir is one of the bestselling premium red wines made in Ontario. It has funky, rich beet, and plum-laden flavours and more tannins than you'd expect in a popular seller. When Ottawa's daily newspaper, the *Citizen*, asked its readers to taste-test the 2002 Henry of Pelham Baco Noir (a vintage that gave the wine qualities reminiscent of a wine from the northern Rhône), hundreds did so. They came up with an average score of four stars out of five.

A reserve level of Baco Noir from the lower-cropped vines is bigger and more intense and has been compared to a Barolo from northern Italy. It does well in competitions when it's tasted blind, but there's still a great deal of prejudice against hybrids. Henry of Pelham's Cabernet-Merlot blends are also noteworthy, and there's a very good range of whites, including Chardonnay, Sauvignon Blanc, Pinot Blanc, and Riesling. The Specks are happy with the way Riesling does in Niagara and wish it were more popular. Daniel Speck says, "We can make a very good Chardonnay, but it's ubiquitous. I wish the industry would get behind Riesling the way New Zealand did with Sauvignon Blanc."

Then there's the Henry of Pelham Rosé, made by the *saignée* method with little skin contact. Made from Pinot Noir, Gamay, Zweigelt, and the Bordeaux reds, it's predictably complex, with bright fruit and berry flavours and some earthy notes. It's also an electrifying pink colour, quite unlike any other Niagara rosé. Daniel Speck, the winery's marketing brain, knows that there's still resistance to rosé wines by male consumers, and he suggests (perhaps optimistically) that Henry of Pelham's version is a "manly pink."

Some experiments just didn't fly. In 2002, Giesbrecht made a port-style wine from Cabernet Franc. It had an opulent texture, with luscious complex, dried fruit flavours. Mindful that the name "port" is meant to be restricted to fortified wines made in the Douro region of Portugal, Henry of Pelham called their port-style wine Fronto—because Henry of Pelham's most successful wine is Baco.

SPRAYING VINES

The most recent development at Henry of Pelham is a line of super-premium wines under the Speck Family Reserve label. It comes in Riesling, Chardonnay, Pinot Noir, and Cabernet-Merlot, and each wine is made only in years that produce fruit that reaches the quality the line demands. The first vintage was 2002 and all lived up to their promise. The Pinot Noir went through an early green harvest, and the grapes that were retained were left hanging until they started to shrivel. The result was a concentrated Pinot with rich, ripe tannins.

There's a real sense of family at Henry of Pelham, and it's one of only a few Niagara wineries that can trace ownership of the land to the 18th century. Stones behind the winery, at the edge of the vineyards, mark the graves of Nicholas Smith's wife and some of their children,

**RIESLING IS ONE OF ONTARIO'S
MOST SUCCESSFUL VARIETIES**

OPPOSITE: **ICEWINE GRAPES NETTED AGAINST BIRDS**

PAGES 102–03: **A VINEYARD IN WINTER**

including Henry, who built the inn that's now at
the winery's heart. The Speck brothers are doing
their ancestors proud.

THE WINERIES

Cave Spring Cellars
3836 Main Street
Jordan, ON L0R 1S0
Tel: 905-562-3581
www.cavespringcellars.com

Creekside Estate Winery
2170 Fourth Avenue
Jordan, ON L0R 1S0
Tel: 905-562-0035
www.creeksideestatewinery.com

Featherstone Estate Winery & Vineyard
3678 Victoria Avenue
Vineland, ON L0R 2C0
Tel: 905-562-1949
www.featherstonewinery.ca

Flat Rock Cellars
2727 Seventh Avenue
Jordan, ON L0R 1S0
Tel: 905-562-8994
www.flatrockcellars.com

Harbour Estates Winery
4362 Jordan Road
Jordan Station, ON L0R 1S0
Tel: 905-562-6279
www.hewwine.com

Harvest Estate Wines
1607 Eighth Avenue
St. Catharines, ON L2R 6P7
Tel: 905-682-0080
www.harvestwines.com

Henry of Pelham Family Estate Winery
1469 Pelham Road
St. Catharines, ON L2R 6P7
Tel: 905-684-8423
www.henryofpelham.com

Hernder Estate Wines
1607 Eighth Avenue
St. Catharines, ON L2R 6P7
Tel: 905-684-3300
www.hernder.com

Kacaba Vineyards
3550 King Street
Vineland, ON L0R 2C0
Tel: 905-562-5625
www.kacaba.com

Lakeview Cellars Estate Winery
4037 Cherry Avenue
Vineland, ON L0R 2C0
Tel: 905-562-5685
www.lakeviewcellars.ca

Le Clos Jordanne
2540 South Service Road
Jordan, ON L0R 1S0
Tel: 905-562-9404

Ridgepoint Wines
3900 Cherry Avenue
Vineland, ON L0R 2C0
Tel: 905-562-8853
www.ridgepointwines.com

Rockway Glen Golf Course & Estate Winery
3290 Ninth Street
St. Catharines, ON L2R 6P7
Tel: 905-641-1030
www.rockwayglen.com

Stoney Ridge Estate Winery
3201 King Street
Vineland, ON L0R 2C0
Tel: 905-562-1324
www.stoneyridge.com

THE WINERIES

Tawse Winery
3955 Cherry Avenue
Vineland, ON L0R 2C0
Tel: 905-562-9500
www.tawsewinery.ca

Thirteenth Street Winery
3983 Thirteeth Street
Jordan Station, ON L0R 1S0
Tel: 905-562-9463
www.13thstreetwines.com

Vineland Estates Winery
3620 Moyer Road
Vineland, ON L0R 2C0
Tel: 905-562-7088
www.vineland.com

Willow Heights Estate Winery
3751 King Street
Vineland, ON L0R 2C0
Tel: 905-562-4945
www.willowheightswinery.com

NIAGARA-ON-THE-LAKE: ST. DAVID'S BENCH, NIAGARA RIVER, AND LAKESHORE

"YOU'VE GOT TO HAVE A LOT OF LOVE FOR THE [PINOT NOIR] GRAPE TO GIVE IT ALL THE ATTENTION IT NEEDS."

—NATALIE REYNOLDS
HILLEBRAND ESTATES WINERY

Niagara-on-the-Lake is the Niagara Peninsula's biggest wine region, extending from the Welland Canal in the west to the Niagara River in the east. The plain between Lake Ontario and the Niagara escarpment is broader here than in the Beamsville, Vineland, and Jordan districts. The area's 22 wineries form three distinct clusters: one on St. David's Bench under the Escarpment, another strung along the Niagara River, and a third lying back from the main town, historic Niagara-on-the-Lake. Except for those on the Bench, almost all are situated on low-lying, relatively flat terrain.

THE WINERIES OF ST. DAVID'S BENCH

Niagara College Teaching Winery

One of Niagara's best-kept secrets is, at the same time, one of its highest-profile wineries. The Niagara College Teaching Winery was nominated for "Winery of the Year" in 2003, and its consistently high-quality wines win acclaim. Yet it falls below the radar of most Ontario wine lovers, and its wines are found on few restaurant lists in wine-savvy cities like Toronto and Ottawa. There are reasons for this paradox. The wines are made by students in College-owned facilities from grapes grown

OPPOSITE: **ONTARIO'S WINE ROUTES ARE WELL MARKED**

in College-owned vineyards. Production is small, about 3,500 cases a year. Although it's happy to win awards and praise, which only serve to showcase the success of its program, the College winery is wary of competing with other Ontario wineries. It promotes itself discreetly and, when a College wine does find a place on a wine list at the expense of an existing listing, the College makes an effort to see that the wine it dislodges is an imported one, not one from Ontario.

The Niagara College Teaching Winery is located on the campus of Niagara College, close to the Queen Elizabeth Way. The winery facilities are in a barn next to some of the vineyards, and the wine retail store is outside the College restaurant—which carries a good selection of the College wines as well as wines from other wineries in the region.

Since 2000, the 24 students admitted each year to the Viticulture and Oenology program embark on a 30-month course of study in viticulture, winemaking, and wine sales and marketing. This program ensures that no matter what job they eventually get in the wine industry, they'll have a well-rounded appreciation of all its facets. The aim is to produce graduates with broad practical experience, rather than the theoretical and scientific qualifications offered by other colleges and universities in Ontario. The winemaking component includes not only reds and whites but also icewine, important for Niagara, of course. The sales and marketing syllabus includes retailing, the LCBO system, and labelling. For viticultural training, students work in three vineyards. The program's manager, Steve Gill, says, "their classroom is 38 acres." The course also includes a four-month internship with an Ontario winery, and graduates of the program are increasingly to be found throughout Ontario's wine industry.

Jim Warren, a part-time instructor and Niagara's best-known winemaker, is one of the keys to the success of the Niagara College Teaching Winery. He was a founder of the current Stoney Ridge winery and has consulted for many others, but his first career was teaching. His efforts and those of the other instructors come to fruition not only in train-

ing another generation of wine professionals but also in the College's unique wine production. This is the only teaching winery in Canada, and revenue from the sale of the College wines goes back to support the program and its operations.

There are about a dozen wines in the portfolio. They include College White (a blend of Vidal, Riesling, and Muscat) and two superb Chardonnays, both in classic Burgundian styles and showing the influence of Jim Warren. Niagara College Sauvignon Blanc has established a reputation as one of the best in the Niagara Peninsula, and it has a lot of competition. As for the reds, Pinot Noir proved outstanding in several years, and the Meritage (Cabernet Franc, Cabernet Sauvignon, and Merlot) often offers complexity and good aging potential. Niagara College Teaching Winery might promote itself discreetly, but its wines speak for themselves, and the awards reaffirm their message. Wine lovers in the know quickly snap up the limited volumes of Sauvignon Blanc and Pinot Noir, and as long as this situation prevails, the winery will remain the best least-known winery in Ontario.

Coyote's Run Estate Winery

A relative newcomer to the Niagara landscape, Coyote's Run might be thought to be cashing in on the fashion of branding wines with cute animals like koala bears, possums, cats, dogs, and wallabies. But the critter on the Coyote's Run label has authenticity: a coyote trail runs along the property. At dusk you can see coyotes hunting mice in the fields, and at night you can hear their yip-yip calls as they keep track of one another.

The vineyard was farmed and the grapes sold to wineries by the Murdza family for 30 years until they opened Coyote's Run. Their first vintage was 2003 and the winery opened the following year. The vines are managed by Steven Murdza, and the winemaker is David Sheppard, who worked at Inniskillin for more than 20 years. Coyote's Run is located at the foot of St. David's Bench in a particularly warm microclimate. The temperature during the growing season is two to three degrees higher than other parts of the Peninsula, especially areas nearer the cooling effects of Lake Ontario. Their grapes ripen sooner and achieve a high level of concentration, and Coyote's Run typically harvests a week or two earlier than most wineries.

The Coyote's Run vineyards are planted with reds like Cabernet Sauvignon, Cabernet Franc, Merlot, Pinot Noir, and Shiraz, and whites that include Chardonnay, Pinot Gris, and Vidal. They source Riesling from other producers in the region. Pinot Noir is getting a lot of attention here because Sheppard is convinced of its potential in their soil. Or, rather, their *soils*, because there are two distinct types in the vineyard: the southeastern part of the vineyard has the fairly heavy black clay that's common in the Niagara Peninsula, while the northwestern half has lighter, red clay, reminiscent in appearance to the terra rossa soil found in Australia's Coonawarra wine region.

Sheppard found that in 2003, Coyote's Run's first vintage, the Pinot Noir delivered different wine, depending on which soil the vines grew in. Vines growing in the dark soil tended to grow small grapes ("They look like blueberries," Sheppard says) that produced a rich and earthy wine with a lot of flavour. The Pinot Noir from vines in the red soil was fruitier and aromatic, and gave more on the nose. In the winery's cellar, the barrels of Pinot Noir are marked "Red Paw" and "Black Paw" in recognition of the coyotes and according to the kind of soil the vines grew in. The wine from the different soil blocks is bottled separately.

Stylistically, Sheppard leans toward Burgundy for his Pinot Noirs and Chardonnays, and an Old World character underlies all of his wine. He describes his preferred style of Pinot Noir as "feminine," not a descriptor you hear much outside France. For him, Pinot Noir in the Oregon style is

NEW SPRING GROWTH

NETTED VINES

"too much of everything," and he hopes it isn't the trend. In the end, he says, "I make wine in the style I like, and I hope enough other people like them, too." It looks as if the winery will make its mark with Pinot Noir and Cabernet Franc. The first vintage of Cabernet Franc won gold and silver medals when it was only a few months old.

Maleta Estate Winery

Maleta Estate Winery occupies a 15-acre (six-hectare) site running down a north-facing ridge near St. David's. Stan and Marilyn Maleta, who are no longer with the winery, bought what was then a run-down vineyard in 1998. At the time, Stan Maleta owned an automobile franchise in Oakville and had been an amateur winemaker for many years. Maleta

Estate was his move into commercial winemaking, and he started making wine in the distinctive pink Quonset hut on the property in 1999. He started on a high note: his off-dry 1999 Reserve Riesling was one of the top 10 wines (and the only non-German wine) among the 1,700 entered in the International Riesling Competition in Germany in 2000.

In January 2004, the winery was purchased by Cadenza Wines Inc., a company operated by Daniel Pambianchi. He's an accomplished amateur winemaker who has written books on home winemaking and is technical editor of *WineMaker* magazine. Asked where his passion for wine comes from, Pambianchi answers simply, "I'm Italian!" As far back as he can remember, he helped his father make wine, and he has relatives involved in the wine business in Italy's Marches wine region. After 20 years as a telecom engineer, Pambianchi wanted to pursue his "real passion of making wine on a commercial basis," and he looked for an opportunity to invest in a winery. With a winemaker who had also started as an amateur, Maleta seemed to be a good match.

The Maletas left the winery in mid-2005, and Arthur Harder joined as consultant winemaker. Harder graduated from the prestigious German oenology college in Geisenheim. He has made wine in Germany and has worked at Inniskillin, Hillebrand, and Ridgepoint. There has been no break with the Maleta style, and the winery's signature wines remain the same. Riesling is a key for Maleta Estate, but Meritage is their flagship. Even so, Pambianchi admits, "the Gamay is so beautiful, it's my personal favourite."

The Gamay was planted in 1969, making it one of the earlier parcels of this variety in Niagara. Other varieties in the Maleta vineyard include Riesling, Chardonnay, Cabernet Sauvignon, Cabernet Franc, and Merlot, all planted between 1969 and 1972. Syrah was added in 1999 and the first vintage was 2002. Maleta Estate currently produces 2,000 cases of wine and plans to double that in the next few years. They released a new wine in 2005, a Pinot Noir from the 2003 vintage, and plan to introduce a sparkling wine and a Riesling icewine.

Château des Charmes

Château des Charmes is a winery you can't miss as you drive along York Road just west of St. David's. In the middle of their manicured vineyards, the Bosc family have built a Loire-style château that doesn't look out of place against the Escarpment. It's a prominent landmark that reflects the long-term contribution the Bosc family has made to Ontario wine.

The roots of the Bosc family go back many generations to Alsace, but their Canadian experience originated, paradoxically, in Algeria. Paul Bosc was managing a winery there when the country gained its independence from France in 1962. The Bosc family left the country and returned to France with little more than they could carry. Like many French citizens who left Algeria at that time, the Boscs didn't feel at home in France, and the family moved

to Montreal in 1963, where Bosc worked briefly as a quality controller at the SAQ, the Québec liquor board. When Bosc contacted one Niagara producer, Château-Gai, and offered some free advice, they promptly offered him a position, and for 15 years he was winemaker and head of research for the winery.

HARVESTING THE VINTAGE

Ontario wine was almost entirely made from labrusca and hybrid varieties in the mid-1960s, and Bosc was one of the few individuals who believed in the potential of Niagara for cultivating vinifera. He encouraged Château-Gai to replant and, more important over the long term, bought himself some land on St. David's Bench. In 1978, Bosc planted a 60-acre (24-hectare) vineyard, which was then the largest single vinifera vineyard in Ontario. Although other plantings were getting underway in the late 1970s, Bosc was so far out in front that by 1981 not only did his vines represent a fifth of all the vinifera in Ontario, but his was the first exclusively vinifera vineyard in the province.

Château des Charmes now has 275 acres (110 hectares) of vines on four sites in Niagara, the largest winery-owned vineyard in Niagara. It's

109

planted in 14 different varieties, but the Burgundian grapes are prominent. Bosc saw in Niagara many similarities to Burgundy, where he himself had studied viticulture and winemaking before working in Algeria. It influenced him toward the Burgundian varieties that Château des Charmes has become noted for: Pinot Noir, Chardonnay, Gamay, and Aligoté. Other varieties represent other regions of France, including Alsace (Riesling, Gewürztraminer, Auxerrois), and Bordeaux (the Cabernets, Merlot, and Sauvignon Blanc).

The French influence is also evident in the style of the château, which was built in 1994, and in the name of the winery. Charmes has a variety of meanings, but here it echoes the way the word is used in Burgundy, as a variation of the word *chaumes*, furrows made by a plow in cultivated ground. To Anglophone ears and eyes, Charmes means charm, and there's no harm in associating the winery with charming wine.

Paul Bosc and Château des Charmes have established a number of landmarks in the development of Ontario wine. Bosc developed the only vinifera clone propagated in Canada and was granted International Plant Breeder's Rights for his Gamay Noir Droit. In 1982, he noticed that one of his Gamay vines was growing differently from the others. It was much taller and its shoots grew upright (*droit*). Gamay Noir Droit ripens later than Gamay and has higher sugar. It makes a wine with noticeably deeper colour and higher alcohol than normally found in Gamay, and the flavours are more concentrated.

Another landmark was the gold medal awarded to the 1990 Paul Bosc Estate Vineyard Chardonnay

VINES IN WINTER

at Vinexpo, France's most prestigious wine exhibition, in 1993. Canadian icewines had won gold at Vinexpo before, but this was the first Canadian table wine to do so. It was an important step in international recognition of the potential of Canadian vineyards to produce quality wine from grapes that hadn't frozen.

Paul Bosc Sr., who was inducted into the Order of Canada in 2005, lives across the road from the château and spends some of his time with his Egyptian Arabian horses. But he's still fully engaged in Château des Charmes, especially the winemaking. His son Paul-André manages the winery, and his other son, Pierre-Jean, was winemaker until 2004. Paul Bosc Sr. then resumed winemaking, with the assistance of Anna Maruggi, who has been with the winery since 1994.

Château des Charmes wines seem to go from strength to strength. They're divided into three lines, one simply known by the name of the winery and two by vineyards: the St. David's Bench Vineyard, which surrounds the château, and the Paul Bosc Estate Vineyard, across York Road from the château. The flagship wine is Equuleus, named for the Little Horse constellation that is visible at harvest and also for Paul Bosc's passion for his Egyptian Arabians. It's a big, saturated blend of Cabernet Sauvignon, Cabernet Franc, and Merlot. Before 1998, Equuleus was labelled Paul Bosc Estate Vineyard Cabernet, and under both labels it has been made only in vintages that produce grapes of high enough quality. Since it was first produced in 1988, five vintages (1992, 1996, 1999, 2000, and 2003) have failed the test.

NIAGARA RIVER

Frogpond Farm

You know you're at a different kind of winery as you park facing a fenced-in run containing hens, a rooster, geese, and sheep, all contributing sound effects not usually associated with a vineyard and winery. But then, Frogpond Farm is a winery with a difference, because it's Niagara's only completely organic vineyard and winery.

FROGPOND FARM WINERY

The owners, Jens Gemmrich and Heike Koch, came to Canada in 1994 from Germany. Gemmrich, who makes the wine, grew up in a Stuttgart grape-growing family and trained as a cooper. He was making wine at Stonechurch when they bought a run-down 10-acre (four-hectare) fruit farm and planted it in 1998 with Riesling, Merlot, and Cabernet Franc. They took a first crop in 2001 and in 2004 opened a retail store. Originally, Gemmrich thought of continuing with a full-time job, but the vineyard demanded too much time, and he now devotes his time to his own winery. He and Koch have now leased another 20 acres (8 hectares), which is planted with Cabernet Franc, Chardonnay, Gamay, Vidal, and Chambourcin.

Gemmrich is quiet spoken and dedicated to his project. He explains that the decision to go organic was as much for personal reasons as any. When they first discussed growing grapes, Heike says,

"With young children in our family, we're not going to spray our vines." They farm the leased vineyard organically, too, but there's a three-year transition period from the last application of a prohibited substance before it can be certified organic.

At present, Frogpond (named for an artificial pond surrounded by bulrushes and inhabited by frogs) produces only three wines: two Rieslings and a Cabernet-Merlot blend. The Riesling comes in un-oaked and oaked styles, but the oaking is gentle because they use big old Germanic 2,500-litre ovals, rather than barriques. The ovals give the Riesling some complexity and texture, without sacrificing any of the citrus zestiness of the un-oaked version. The red blends, too, are fruity, without any interference from the barrels.

All Frogpond wines are in 500-mL bottles. Like the organic label, this sets Frogpond wines off from the competition, but restaurants also like the half-litre format and Gemmrich says it's ideal for couples who want more than a half bottle but don't want to drink a standard bottle of wine. Gemmrich and Koch aim to make about 2,500 cases of wine in all, but the first few years have been tough. There were good crops in 2001 and 2002, but no crop at all in 2003 and only half-crops in 2004 and 2005. Being organic means that, unlike other wineries, they can't purchase grapes from other growers when their own vines don't deliver. And it's not only the wines that are organic. Even the souvenir ball caps, with Frogpond's eye-catching logo, are made from organic cotton.

This is a small, attractive winery with a difference. Gemmrich and Koch negotiate the work between them: she pours tastes for visitors while he takes a wine writer on a tour of the vineyard; then he looks after the tasting bar while she takes a group of tourists to the winemaking facilities.

Riverview Cellars Estate Winery

Riverview Cellars Estate Winery is located on one of the region's busiest roads in summer, the Niagara Parkway. The owner is Sam Pillitteri, brother of Gary Pillitteri who established Pillitteri Estates. Unlike Gary, who gravitated quickly to Niagara on com-

ing to Canada, Sam first lived in Halifax, where he ran a pizzeria. In 1975, he and his wife, Lina, traded cheese for trees, and bought a 25-acre (10-hectare) fruit farm near the Niagara River.

When the great vinifera planting boom began, Sam Pillitteri leapt on board. He began to introduce vines (Gewürztraminer first) in 1990 and, by 2000, what had been an orchard had become a vineyard. The winery opened the same year. Now the nine varieties (seven vinifera and two hybrid) contribute to a portfolio of table and dessert wines (select late harvest and icewine made from Vidal). The winemaker since 2004 has been Fred Di Profio, a graduate of Brock University's oenology and viticulture program.

Dessert wines have proved very successful for Riverview Cellars and so have sweeter table wines. Riverview makes a semisweet Vidal (registering 3 on the LCBO sugar scale) and a similarly sweet red, which is their biggest-selling wine. Called Fontana Dolce, it's a blend of 50 percent Cabernet Sauvignon, 30 percent Merlot, and 20 percent Baco Noir. It's recommended not only for drinking but also as a base for Sangria. It's possible that Riverview's American customers boost demand for the sweeter wines. Riverview is on the main tourist route, has the only website that gives prices in both Canadian and U.S. dollars, and also ships to all states in the U.S. Most of Riverview's table wines are varietals, but there's also a Meritage. The flagship wine is Salvatore's Cabernet Franc Reserve (Salvatore is Sam Pillitteri's real name), made only in years that produce fruit of high enough quality.

Marynissen Estates

Concession One runs parallel to the Niagara Parkway, and there you find Marynissen Estates. It was founded by John Marynissen, who immigrated to Canada from the Netherlands in 1952 and bought a farm, now the vineyards. He not only grew apples and grapes but also raised pigs on the property. Sandra Marynissen, his daughter and now the winemaker, says her father and the farm graduated from "swine to wine."

OPPOSITE: **ROSES GROW AT THE END OF THE VINE**

All the grapes planted in the early 1950s were hybrids, but Marynissen developed an interest in wine that went beyond them. With no formal training, he became an avid and award-winning amateur winemaker and is one of the three winemakers (along with Jim Warren and Eddy Gurinskas) who from the mid-1990s have made their own lots of Pinot Noir for sale in boxed sets under the Three Guys label.

NETTING ICEWINE GRAPES AGAINST BIRDS

When Niagara vineyards began the shift from hybrids to vinifera in the 1970s, Marynissen was one of the first to replace most of his vines. In 1978, the year he was elected Grape King, Marynissen planted Chardonnay and Gamay, and in the face of prevailing wisdom that the variety wouldn't survive in Niagara, he also planted Cabernet Sauvignon. His vines are now thought to be the oldest Cabernet Sauvignon in Canada. He sold his grapes to wineries and might have continued doing so if Sandra Marynissen, who became increasingly involved in the vineyards during the 1980s, hadn't encouraged her father to set up his own winery. In 1990, they made their first vintage, and they opened the winery the following year.

Marynissen's insistence on planting Cabernet Sauvignon in the 1970s turned out to be a sign of what was to come. About a third of the winery's 70 acres (28 hectares) of vines are in that variety, with the remainder in about a dozen other varieties, ranging from Sauvignon Blanc and Viognier to Gamay and Petite Sirah. They produce 10,000 cases in a good year, like 2002, but recent cold winters reduced output to as little as 2,000 cases in 2003.

Big reds are the favourites in Marynissen's stable, with Cabernet Sauvignon to the fore. The Cabernet Sauvignons from good vintages are big-bodied, tannic, and flavoursome, and can pack up to 14 percent alcohol, which is high by Niagara standards. The Cabernet-Merlot blends are also weighty, with plenty of fruit to last out the firm tannins. Both of these wines have very good cellaring potential. A different Bordeaux blend combines Malbec (75 percent) and Cabernet Franc (25 percent) to make a fruit-rich red with drying tannins.

As if to signal the Marynissens' attraction to Bordeaux, at the back of the tasting bar stands an empty bottle of 1975 Château Lascombes, a second-growth in the 1855 Bordeaux classification. Sandra Marynissen and her husband, Glenn Muir, drank it to celebrate when they completed their sommelier training. But it's not all Bordeaux. Marynissen also produces successful Gamay in both oaked and un-oaked styles, as well as attractive Pinot Gris and Chardonnay.

Inniskillin

Several stylish, multimillion dollar wineries have appeared on the Niagara landscape in the last few years, but some of the region's stellar wineries are housed in much more modest quarters. One is Inniskillin, whose vineyards lie on the Niagara Parkway. For Inniskillin, "it's always been about vineyards, not added landscape," says its co-founder, Donald Ziraldo. The centre of the complex of buildings at Inniskillin is the Brae Burn barn, built in the 1920s in a design influenced by Frank Lloyd Wright. On its main floor is the wine store and visitors' centre and on the second a gallery documents the history of the winery.

**THE BRAE BURN BARN
AT INNISKILLIN**

Ziraldo and his partner, Karl Kaiser, found their inspiration to start a winery in a bottle of wine in the early 1970s. Ziraldo, who has a degree in agriculture from the University of Guelph, was running the family nursery that specialized in fruit trees and grape vines. "One fateful day," Ziraldo writes in his book on Inniskillin, *Anatomy of a Winery*, "Karl bought some French hybrid grapevines from me at the nursery and, some time afterward, we shared a bottle of Karl's homemade wine." Kaiser had a degree in chemistry and was an avid amateur winemaker. "After a lot of dreaming and talking, we decided to apply for a wine licence."

Getting that licence was the first of Inniskillin's achievements, for it inaugurated the most recent chapter in Niagara's wine history. In 1974, the Liquor Licensing Board of Ontario granted "Donald Zaraldo" of the "Inniskillian" winery a licence to make 450 gallons of wine "for tasting purposes and for submission to the Liquor Control Board

of Ontario." The original copy of this badly-typed licence, with the names of both Inniskillin and Donald Ziraldo misspelled, is a historic document. It was the first new commercial wine licence issued in Ontario since 1929, and it now hangs in the upper level of the Brae Burn barn.

The first vintages were made in a packing shed at the Ziraldo nursery, a couple of kilometres from the present winery's location. For the name of their winery they chose Inniskillin, after the Inniskillin Farm the nursery was located on. It had been so named by a colonel in the Inniskilling Fusiliers, who had been granted the land after serving in the War of 1812. Within a couple of years, though, Inniskillin outgrew those facilities, and in 1978 it relocated to the Brae Burn Estate, where it is today. The vineyard at the winery is named Brae Burn after the estate,

HARVESTED GRAPES

and Americans when they think of icewine. Its pre-eminence was recognized when Riedel, the bench-mark wineglass producer based in Austria, used Inniskillin icewine to design a glass specifically for icewine. It's in Riedel's Vinum Extreme series.

Karl Kaiser has made the icewine since 1984, and it was he who made the 1989 Vinexpo winner and quickly established Inniskillin's name as a leading producer. Perhaps Kaiser's Austrian heritage point-ed him toward icewine—it was initially a German wine, but has been made for centuries in Austria. Although many aficionados prefer Riesling icewine because of its high natural acidity, Kaiser is espe-cially pleased with his icewines made from Vidal, a hybrid variety. Many Germans and Austrians are jealous of Canada's ability to use Vidal, he says, because European wine laws don't permit the use of hybrids. He likes the tropical flavours you get out of Vidal, compared to the more citrus and peach flavours in Riesling icewine.

Kaiser can come across as fairly dour, but he's adventurous in the winery. Many styles have become known as "Karl's experiments," and not all saw the light of the commercial market. One that did, but only for a short time, is a red icewine made from Dornfelder, a German cross. Kaiser made ice-wine from Dornfelder in 1997, 1998, and 1999, then stopped for commercial reasons: "The marketing didn't work." Dornfelder icewine is expensive ($200 a 375-mL bottle) and exquisite. Kaiser describes it as "more like port, without the alcohol." (Dornfelder icewine has 10 percent alcohol.)

Other Kaiser successes include sparkling ice-wine. It's a style that sets some professionals' teeth on edge, but Kaiser likes it a lot. The bubbles have the effect of lightening the sweetness to some extent (and making the wine more food-friendly), but the Vidal's tropical flavours still come through clearly.

Donald Ziraldo is the face of Inniskillin. Various identities swirl around him—jet-set playboy, inter-national wine salesman, company ambassador at wine shows around the world—and he's the first person the media seek out for views on Ontario wine and wine in general. In 2005 he was quoted

and the original vineyard, the Seeger vineyard, is adjacent. There's another vineyard, Klose, in this area near the Niagara River, while a fourth, Montague Estate vineyard, lies closer to Lake Ontario. The total 130 acres (50 hectares) of vines contribute to Inniskillin's output of 120,000 cases a year.

Inniskillin, which helped create the big Vincor wine company, set the pace for the development of the modern Ontario wine industry. It established a name for itself and Ontario early on by winning medals in prestigious international competitions. The first of these came in 1991, when Inniskillin's 1989 Vidal icewine won the top medal, the Grand Prix d'Honneur, at Vinexpo, France's most impor-tant wine competition.

Even now, when the Ontario wine scene is a lot more crowded, Inniskillin's icewine has widespread international recognition. Inniskillin is the name that first comes to the lips of Europeans, Asians, as saying it was difficult to get a decent French wine under $25. It provoked SOPEXA, a company promoting French wine in Canada, into putting on a tasting of 80 sub-$25 French wines to test Ziraldo's assessment. Ziraldo attended the tasting and seemed surprised that one of his comments (which he couldn't remember making) had given rise to an event well attended by the wine media and by the French trade commissioner. After tasting the wines, Ziraldo readily admitted he was wrong. Not many Ontario wine personalities can count on their throw-away comments being taken so seriously.

Inniskillin's winemaker for many years was Australian Philip Dowell, but in 2004 he returned to Australia. His place was taken by James Manners, also an Australian, who came to Inniskillin from Poet's Corner Winery in New South Wales. Manners arrived at the end of the 2004 harvest, just in time to take over the final stages of that vintage's winemak-

ing and to see the wines through their maturation. What is it like to take over wine that another winemaker has supervised up to that point? Manners has an unattractive comparison: "It's like looking after someone else's dirty underpants." If that sounds a bit negative, the rest of what Manners has to say corrects it. "I think Niagara Peninsula is a really amazing area. I like it because it's a bit of a challenge, and the big challenge is to get the fruit right."

He has ideas for some of Inniskillin's staple varieties. Manners likes the Pinot Noirs, like the very successful Montague Estate Vineyard, but would like to make it more complex, "a bit more left of centre." He also wants to take Niagara Pinot Gris in a more complex direction. Curiously for an Australian, Manners isn't a big fan of Shiraz/Syrah. His favourite variety to work with is Merlot—a

THE BRAE BURN BARN AT INNISKILLIN

preference he attributes jokingly to the fact that his mother is not only French but from Bordeaux. Merlot is Bordeaux's most widely-planted grape variety and, Manners observes, "It's genetic for people from Bordeaux to hate Pinot Noir." Of Merlot he says, "I want to get it right before I die. It's my Pinot Noir," a reference to the fact that many winemakers throw up their hands in despair at Pinot Noir, a notoriously fickle grape in the vineyard and in the winery.

Manners is also having to adapt to a region where Cabernet Franc does very well. In Australia, Cabernet Franc has practically disappeared, and it's considered "a cockroach of a vine." He was horrified when he did a blind tasting in Niagara and found that the wine he liked most was a Cabernet Franc.

James Manners is quickly making his imprint on Inniskillin. He's tackling the long-standing tensions between Niagara wineries and the growers who provide grapes on a contract basis. Apart from the to-be-expected issues surrounding prices, many growers have felt they didn't get enough recognition for their work. Soon after arriving at Inniskillin, Manners started holding post-harvest meetings with growers to taste wines and discuss disease management and yields.

It will be interesting to watch the transition from one winemaker to another at Inniskillin. The winery's successful style won't change overnight, but winemakers always put their mark on their wine, and Manners clearly has a sense of the direction he wants to push some of his wines. Any transition is bound to be gradual, for Inniskillin's range of wines has a popular following. Inniskillin is well represented on LCBO shelves and also sells at Vincor's Wine Rack stores. Among the notable wines are the Single Vineyard and Founders' Reserve series.

Reif Estate Winery

If many of Ontario's winery owners are new to the business, others are old hands, at least in terms of lineage. One of the oldest must be the Reif family: Klaus Reif, president of Reif Estate, is the 13th generation of his family to grow grapes and make wine. The earliest family records of grape growers go back to 1638 in Neustadt, in Germany's Pfalz wine region.

Klaus grew up at the family winery, Weingut Reif in Germany. He might have taken it over in due course, but he discovered the New World when, at the age of 15, he and his father visited his uncle Ewald, who had planted a vineyard on the Niagara property where Reif Estate now stands. They tasted some of the wines being made at that time (1978), but weren't impressed. "They were . . . not up to expectations, let's phrase it that way," says Klaus. Klaus' father looked around at the soil, the climate, at Toronto with three million people not so far away, at Niagara Falls, and said, "We should open a winery."

Klaus' Uncle Ewald was keen to grow grapes and was hesitant about being diverted by a winery, but he was soon persuaded. He went into partnership with Klaus' father and started making wine in 1982, got a licence in 1983, and opened to the public the same year. It was agreed that Ewald would run the winery for a few years and that his brother and nephews would then take it over. The responsibility fell on Klaus, who graduated from Germany's premier wine school at Geisenheim in 1987, with degrees in both oenology and viticulture. Two weeks later, at the age of 24, he travelled to Niagara-on-the-Lake and took over the running of the winery his uncle had opened four years earlier.

The next year, 1988, Reif offered a four-month co-op internship to a student in microbiology and fermentation technologies at the University of Guelph. Roberto DiDomenico was the son of Italian immigrants to Canada, and his introduction to wine was helping his father make their own wine each fall. The internship obviously worked for both men. When Roberto graduated in 1989, he was hired as Reif's winemaker and, since that time, both men have collaborated in making Reif Estates' wines.

It's been a long partnership and, they say, a good one. "It was kind of fun," DiDomenico says about their start together. "Klaus and I are about the same age—well, Klaus is older, obviously!—and he had young, fresh ideas, and I was fresh out of university.

NEW GROWTH

There were only 10 or 15 wineries at the time, and people were trying different things." A few years ago, the friendly competition between these two men with German and Italian backgrounds took the form of a taste-off that compared German and Italian sausages.

Reif's 135 acres (54 hectares) are planted in 15 varieties and provide more grapes than the winery needs for its annual production of 35,000 cases. Typically they sell some of their grapes to other wineries, including one in Prince Edward County. As you'd expect of a German-owned winery, Riesling table wines are important, but Reif has also made a name for itself with reds, especially Cabernet Merlot and Bordeaux blends. Those varieties make up the largest block of vines going to table wines. The first Bordeaux blend, called Tesoro (Treasure), was produced in 1995, and as the vines have aged, the wines have improved. "The reds are really

starting to show. They were planted in 1988, 1989, and they're really starting to produce much more concentrated fruit and extract," Rob DiDomenico comments.

An important variety for Reif is Vidal, which is primarily destined for late-harvest and icewine. Exports of icewine—made from Vidal, Riesling, Cabernet Franc, and Cabernet Sauvignon—are an important part of the business, bringing in about a fifth of the winery's earnings. There are major icewine exports to Japan, Taiwan, and China.

There have been several experiments. In the early 1990s, they planted a parcel of Zinfandel and used the grapes for light rosés until the 2001 vintage, when it produced a classic red for the first time. But the vines died in the harsh winter of 2002–03. A more recent initiative is the First Growth line of wines, which was launched in 2003 with the 2001 vintage. This is an ultra-premium line of reds that are made to Reif's stringent criteria. The grapes are from the oldest blocks, cropped to two tonnes an acre, hand-picked, and given longer-than-usual two-year barrel-aging. The 2001 First Growth wines (Pinot Noir, Cabernet Franc, and Cabernet Merlot) were all remarkable for their concentration and style.

Lailey Vineyard

Lailey Vineyard is one of the new kids on the block, and, like many new Ontario wineries, it was originally an orchard with a few vines. In the 1970s, the founder's son, David Lailey, and his wife, Donna, planted the present vineyard with the vinifera varieties that were just starting to make their presence known in the region. Lailey Vineyard quickly established a reputation. In 1991, Donna Lailey was acclaimed Niagara's first Grape Queen; until then, the annual Grape King title, honouring the grower of the year, had been awarded only to men. Also in the 1990s, Southbrook Winery, which bought grapes from Lailey, began to designate Lailey Vineyard on its labels.

Like a number of growers, the Laileys eventually decided to make their own wine, rather than sell their grapes. In 1999, they joined forces with Derek Barnett, who had been making wine for Southbrook. He made the 2000 vintage for Lailey, and in the first years the wine was sold from a cramped store at the back of the family house. The winery officially opened in 2002, and now visitors are welcomed to a tasting bar and retail store in a modern wood building that also houses the winemaking facilities and barrel room. From the second floor there's an excellent view over the vines, mainly Chardonnay and Pinot Noir.

A BUD IN SPRING

Barnett came to grapes via cows. He studied agricultural science in England, with a specialty in dairy farming, before moving to Canada in 1971. For the next 30 years he worked for Southbrook Farms (outside Toronto), which had a large Jersey herd. When Southbrook branched out into wine, in 1991, Barnett tried his hand at making wine. He makes it sound easy: "They needed a winemaker and I said I'd give it a go." Ten years later, he leapt at the opportunity to become a co-owner of Lailey Vineyard winery (which is commercially independent of the vineyards): "It was a simple decision to become part-owner of a small winery in Niagara-on-the-Lake."

For someone trained to manage cows, Barnett is bullish about his wines. He makes many different reds and whites for the Lailey label, but he especially likes working with Chardonnay and Pinot Noir, each for a different reason. Chardonnay, he points out, is "a winemaker's grape." It's one of the most neutral varieties, and allows winemakers to imprint their styles distinctively on the wine. Barnett aims for balance and fruit purity. He makes Chardonnay in a number of styles but generally likes them barrel-fermented (which, contrary to widespread expectation, doesn't produce a heavy oak flavour), with fresh fruit flavours and food-friendly crispness. Niagara's cool climate generally ensures good acidity.

He's optimistic, too, about Pinot Noir, which, he says, is making Lailey's best wine. "It's tough to grow and tough to make, but if you focus on yield and quality, I think Pinot Noir is the variety we should focus on here." He estimates that the weather in Niagara-on-the-Lake is good for Pinot Noir five years out of six. The Laileys have increased their plantings of Pinot Noir, and Barnett makes it in a delicate style more reminiscent of Burgundy than of other New World regions. He's not a big fan of big, fruity Pinot Noirs: "They're not really Pinots." Even before the movie *Sideways* pumped up the market for Pinot Noir, Lailey's were flying off the shelves, so they're clearly doing something right. Barnett was among the first Ontario winemakers to work with barrels made from Canadian oak. Lailey sells Chardonnay, Pinot Noir, and icewine aged in

Canadian oak, and each bottle carries a small gold sticker attesting to the fact.

Lailey is a young winery that has quickly earned a reputation for producing wines of consistent quality. A third generation of Laileys—Donna and David's daughter, Tonya—is already at work in

THE WARM TONES OF WINE-STAINED OAK

the vineyards, and Lailey is moving forward to establish itself as an organic vineyard. Their rapid success is clearly due to the winning combination of first-class fruit and excellent winemaking, and it should ensure that Lailey Vineyard winery goes from strength to strength.

Peller Estates

Peller Estates sits back from the road amid 25 acres (10 hectares) of vines. An elegant château-style building that opened in 2001 houses not only the winery but also a retail store, tasting rooms, and one of the region's best restaurants. This is the prestige face of Andrés Wines, one of Canada's largest wine producers, which makes premium VQA wines, non-VQA Canadian wines, blended Canadian and foreign wines, and juice

ONTARIO WINE COUNTRY SIGN

for home winemakers. Andrés also operates a chain of more than 100 Vineyard Estates Wines' retail stores throughout Ontario.

The company was founded by Andrew Peller, who emigrated from Hungary in the 1920s. He worked in a brewery before starting his own and, in the 1960s, established the Andrés company in Port Moody, British Columbia. Andrés now owns vineyards in British Columbia, Ontario, and Nova Scotia. It isn't clear why Andrew Peller chose the name "Andrés" for his company. It is, of course, a faux-French variation of his own name, and the French connection might well have had some cachet in the 1960s.

In Niagara, Andrés currently owns Peller Estates and Hillebrand Estates, in the middle of the Niagara-on-the Lake area, and Thirty Bench Vineyard and Winery on the Beamsville Bench. The bulk of its wines, though, are produced in a former tobacco plant on the side of the Queen Elizabeth Way in Winona, just west of Beamsville. Peller Estates winemaker, Rob Summers, produces 60,000 cases of wine a year in a number of distinct brands. The highest level is the Andrew Peller Signature series of varietal wines, all made in small lots and limited quantities. They include three red Bordeaux varieties, Chardonnay, Riesling, and Vidal icewine, and all follow a full-fruit style that retains the typicity and complexity of each variety. Cabernet Franc, Riesling, and Chardonnay are particularly solid, vintage after vintage.

The next tier is Peller Private Reserve, which is mostly oak aged and again made in limited quantities. Nine varieties contribute to this line, and notable wines to look for are the Gamay Noir and Pinot Noir. Another series worth noting is the Limited Edition Founder's Series, which are made in volumes of fewer than 1,000 cases.

THE WINERIES OF NIAGARA LAKESHORE

Jackson-Triggs Niagara Estate Winery

Along Niagara Stone Road lies Jackson-Triggs Niagara Estate. Part of the enormous Vincor company, it carries "Niagara" in its name because there's also a Jackson-Triggs Okanagan Estate in British Columbia. Both are named for their founders, Allan Jackson and Don Triggs, and the first vintage of wines bearing the Jackson-Triggs name was 1992. One of the most widely sold Ontario brands, Jackson-Triggs is well represented in the LCBO, and the wines are also sold throughout Ontario in Vincor's Wine Rack retail stores.

The present winery opened in 2001, and it's a standout. From the outside it can look at first rather stark and industrial. But Rob Scapin, Vincor's chief winemaker, is only half-joking when he refers to the structure as "our barn." In part, it's a reference to the Brae Burn barn that's the centrepiece at Inniskillin Wines, a Vincor sibling of Jackson-Triggs. But it's also a recognition that the Jackson-Triggs facility was modelled on a barn. It has post-and-beam-style frames made from steel and Douglas fir, and a façade of glass, stylish stone, and sleek aluminum.

Inside, it's equally impressive, with a variety of fermenters (roto-fermenters, open-top, and conventional tanks) and built on three levels so that gravity moves the wine between the production stages. The winery produces a lot of wine—90,000 cases plus icewine—and the tanks are packed in densely. Even so, the facility gives the impression of airiness and openness.

In two underground rooms, wines age in 1,750 barrels, slightly more French than American, with a smattering of European and Canadian. The Chardonnay and Pinot Noir go into French barrels, the Merlot and Cabernet Franc into American, while the Cabernet Sauvignon goes into both. The barrels are set on gravel to allow a degree of natural coolness and humidity. This is the Burgundian mode, but unlike Burgundian winemakers, Scapin doesn't allow tasters to spit into the gravel. "I guess I'm just too hygienically minded," he laughs. "I'm just too New World. I don't want any bacterial growth in the cellar." There's another consideration: part of the barrel room is set aside for dinners.

The tens of thousands of people who visit the winery each year enter through a wide portal (the "barn-door") with tasting rooms on the left and the winemaking facility to the right. A comprehensive guided tour starts up a long ramp at the back of the building overlooking the vineyards, and continues inside along the winery's top level. Scapin jokes that "So far, there haven't been any issues—kids haven't opened up any valves."

There's a small estate vineyard, but Jackson-Triggs buys 90 percent of its grapes from independent growers on long-term contracts. One of the important sources is the Delaine Vineyard, owned by and named for Donald Triggs (Vincor Global President) and his wife, Elaine. This is a 100-acre vineyard not far from the winery, planted with about 10 different varieties. It produces premium fruit, some of which goes into Jackson-Triggs' excellent Delaine Vineyard series.

What makes Delaine special? Rob Scapin suggests that the location gets the true Niagara River influence, but that the Triggses' attention to the vineyard has also been critical. They've planted very

JACKSON-TRIGGS WINERY

good clones (ripping some out when they weren't performing to expectations and replacing them with others) on a variety of rootstocks, and they're serious about keeping yields down.

Rob Scapin, the winery's first winemaker, came to Jackson-Triggs from Australia in 1998. Educated at Roseworthy College, Australia's famous oenology school, he worked at several wineries, including Brown Brothers in northeastern Victoria. At Jackson-Triggs, he oversaw the design and construction of the new winery and made wine in 1998 and 1999. The following two vintages were made by Scapin and Tom Seaver, a winemaker from California who took over from 2002. Seaver returned to California in mid-2005 to make wine at the huge Gallo winery. Transitions from one winemaker to another in a winery always raise questions of continuity and style in the wines. Every winemaker is expected to put his or her fingerprint on wine, but consumers don't want radical changes in style. The current style of Jackson-Triggs stresses rich, pure fruit and careful balance, and many of the upper-tier wines achieve a high degree of elegance.

Jackson-Triggs markets its wines in several tiers. At the top is the Delaine Vineyard series, including

THE COOL EFFICIENCY OF STAINLESS STEEL
OPPOSITE: **THE WARMTH OF BARRELS**

some remarkable (and well-priced) reds like Merlot, Cabernet Sauvignon, and Pinot Noir. Warm vintages, in particular, offer intense fruit, skilled balance, and very good typicity for each variety. At a similar level is a range of Proprietors' Grand Reserve wines, including a stylish Meritage, which is predominantly Merlot and Cabernet Sauvignon with some Cabernet Franc.

The whites are equally impressive. A lower-tier Proprietors' Reserve Sauvignon Blanc has all the fruit and briskness to reinforce the view that this variety does very well in Niagara. And there's an excellent off-dry Riesling, too, with zesty lime, lemon, melon, and passion fruit flavours. Together with a Cabernet Franc Rosé (new in 2004) and icewines, Jackson-Triggs has an impressive portfolio.

Stratus Vineyards

Stratus Vineyards is a winery built with a purpose, which refers not only to the building and winemaking facilities but also to the very philosophy of wine. Stratus set out to make its name with premium blended wines, not varietals, and the vineyards were planted accordingly. At the same time, no effort (or, it seems, expense) was spared to put together a facility that represents up-to-the-minute technology and sensitivity to the environmental impact of winemaking. Nor were aesthetics ignored. From Niagara Stone Road, Stratus Vineyards has a fairly industrial look, giving an impression similar to the Jackson-Triggs winery that's visible not far away. Inside, the design is stark, with the colour scheme dominated by black and shades of medium to dark grey. But it's all understated elegance. The interior is flooded with natural light. There's a long tasting bar and imposing shelves of Stratus wines, with their sleek, minimalist white, grey, and black labels that, in the best (or worst, depending on your point of view) French tradition, tell you virtually nothing about the wine inside.

Stratus is the creation of a Toronto-based partnership led by David Feldberg, CEO of Teknion, which makes office furniture. Feldberg bought what would become the Stratus Vineyard in 2000 and hired consultants to conceive and design a winery that would establish a unique profile among Niagara wines. They brought on board key personnel from other Niagara wineries, including winemaker Jean-Laurent Groux.

Groux, who hails from the Loire Valley in France, is a genial character who looks like a throwback to the '60s. He has wild hair, a bushy beard, an occasionally manic look to his eyes—a cross between Allen Ginsberg and Albert Einstein, which seems appropriate for the mix of art and science that is winemaking. Groux had been winemaker at Hillebrand Estates since 1989. His reputation grew, particularly for his barrel-fermented icewines and blended wines like the Trius and Trius Grand Reserve series.

In some respects, Stratus' emphasis on blends is hardly a radical approach in the New World

generally and in Ontario specifically. Most wineries produce blends (usually "Bordeaux blends" that include two or all of Cabernet Sauvignon, Merlot, and Cabernet Franc). And many varietally labelled wines are really blends that are labelled with a single variety because they include more than the minimum percentage specified by wine law. (Under Ontario VQA rules, for example, a wine can be labelled Chardonnay as long as it includes at least 85 percent Chardonnay.) Where Stratus is breaking new ground is in making white and red blends—called simply Stratus White and Stratus Red—their flagship wines. The actual varieties and proportions vary from year to year: Groux simply assembles the components to make the best wine each vintage.

The recipes are a secret, although Groux offers tantalizing hints. The 2002 Stratus White, he con-

cedes, includes Chardonnay, Gewürztraminer, Riesling, Semillon, Sauvignon Blanc, and "whatever else fits" the blend. As for the 2002 Stratus Red, it includes Petit Verdot, Syrah, Cabernet Sauvignon, Cabernet Franc, Gamay, Merlot, and Malbec, and "whatever else fits." Groux lists 12 varieties here, and because only 13 are planted in the Stratus vineyards, we can assume that, in 2002 at least, those Stratus wines contained a bit of everything on offer. The real secret, of course, lies in the proportions of each variety in the final blend, and on that, Groux is tight-lipped.

Stratus does produce varietal wines, too, including Chardonnay, Cabernet Franc, and a Riesling icewine. A second label, Wildass, features white and red blends sold exclusively to restaurants.

Where does this preoccupation with blending come from? For Groux, who was born in France, it's a sort of return to the principles of French winemaking, where blending is the norm in some

BRIDGING A CREEK AT KACABA VINEYARDS

of the most prestigious appellations. Bordeaux, whether red or white, are almost always blends, as are Champagnes and Rhône wines, including Châteauneuf-du-Pape. (Burgundy, Alsace, and much of the Loire, on the other hand, tend to make varietal wines.)

The Stratus vineyards comprise about 50 acres (20 hectares), classified into 33 separate blocks so that grapes can be vinified separately by block and variety. The original vineyard was planted with Chardonnay and Cabernet Sauvignon in the late 1970s, during the first vinifera rush, but Stratus has replaced most of those vines. The stress is now on reds associated with Bordeaux and the Rhône, especially Syrah and Petit Verdot. Groux says that Petit Verdot, which is a very minor grape in Bordeaux, does very well in his vineyards.

The vines grow on Scott Henry trellises, which maximize light and air circulation, in clay loam that's high in organic components and is well drained. Stratus practises sustainable viticulture, using no fertilizers and no herbicides. Winter temperatures are moderated by six wind machines, but Stratus is located in one of the warmest microclimates in the Niagara Peninsula, where it benefits from the warming effects of the Niagara River and Lake Ontario. There is, notably, no Pinot Noir in the Stratus vineyards. Says Groux, "I don't believe this is the right place."

Like all winemakers, Groux follows the precept that wine is predominantly made in the vineyard. But by no means does he neglect the winery. The Stratus facility is built on flat land but, right from the start, Groux wanted a gravity-fed winery, one where juice and wine flows from one stage to another without being pumped. Some Niagara wineries, like Malivoire, are able to achieve that by building on a hillside, but Stratus had to innovate. The core of Stratus is a series of elevators that enable tanks to be raised, so that wine can flow from them without artificial assistance.

Beyond that, Stratus's designers tried to minimize its impact on the environment. The building is made of inert materials and is cooled geothermally by 24 wells drilled 230 feet (70 metres) into the

WIND MACHINES ARE WIDELY USED TO MODERATE WINTER TEMPERATURES

ground. Stratus was the first building in Canada to be awarded LEED—Leadership in Energy and Environmental Design—status, granted by the Canada Green Building Council.

Coming out of all this effort and attention to detail are some stunning wines that are winning accolades. Stratus red and white are perfectly poised, complex, and layered. Groux says they parallel the best of the complexity and variety in the vineyard. The varietal wines, too, stand out. They come at a price, though. Most Stratus wines are in the $30 to $40 range, and wine tourists looking for a $10 bottle of wine are out of luck. But for $10, visitors to Stratus can taste a flight of three wines, and looking over the dramatic facility is free.

The Stratus name fits into an international family of cult wines, with names like Opus and Dominus. For wine, it conjures up a little ambivalence, for who wants to buy a cloudy wine (unless it's the iconic New Zealand Sauvignon Blanc, Cloudy Bay)? On the other hand, "stratus" speaks to the soil strata where the vines grow and to clouds that temper the sun, and it suggests that, for this winery, the sky's the limit.

Joseph's Estate Wines

Joseph Pohorly is one of the pioneers of the modern wine industry in Niagara. He grew up in a fruit-farming family in the region and worked as a teacher and an engineer before getting into wine. His first venture, in 1979, was the Newark winery, located on his family's farm. Echoing the former name of Niagara-on-the-Lake, it was only the fourth winery to open in Ontario since the late 1920s. In 1982, Pohorly sold the major share of Newark to a German company, which renamed it Hillebrand. Pohorly stayed on for a while as chief winemaker and president, and in 1983 made one of Niagara's first commercial icewines. He left Hillebrand in 1986 to work as a developer and hotelier, but by then wine was part of his identity, and in 1992 he bought 20 acres (eight hectares) of orchard and planted it in vinifera vines. He produced his wine, a Pinot Gris, in 1995, and opened Joseph's Estate the following year.

For what appears to be a small operation, Joseph's is a big producer. It makes 30,000 cases a year, most from the winery's own grapes, the rest from independent growers. Pohorly is indignant at the share the LCBO takes of the selling price of the wines it carries, so he sells all his wine from his country-style retail store and directly to licensees. "We're in 600 hotels and restaurants from Sault Ste. Marie to Ottawa," he says. In 2004, Joseph's Merlot Reserve was chosen as the official red wine of the Ontario Legislature. "It's funny to watch the MPs coming and tasting the [candidate] wines," Pohorly says. "Some of them knew what they were doing, others brought other people to taste for them. It was an honour to be chosen."

All Joseph's Estate wines are VQA-quality, and they cover a wide range of varieties and styles. Included are a well-made Pinot Noir, with attractive cherry flavours, and wine made from Chancellor, a hybrid variety. Some vintages offer dark fruit flavours with pungent smoke and leather notes. But, given Pohorly's history, it isn't surprising that Vidal icewine is a forte of the winery. He favours Vidal because of its flavour profile and thick skin, and many vintages are classic expressions, with an exacting balance of fruit sweetness and acidity.

Caroline Cellars Winery

Caroline Cellars is one of the newer Lakeshore entries, somewhat isolated in the middle of the countryside along Line 2. It's named for Caroline Lakeit, the late mother and grandmother of the winery's founders. Her maiden name was Hernder, and her brother Fred opened Hernder Estates in Jordan.

Ricky Lakeit Jr., one of Caroline Cellars' owners and one of Caroline Lakeit's grandchildren, is the fifth generation of his family to grow grapes. His great-grandfather immigrated to Canada after World War II and grew grapes in Niagara, and his father bought the land on Line 2 in 1978. The family began to make their own wine in 2000, and two years later they opened the winery building, which houses winemaking facilities, a tasting room, and a loft for functions.

Listening to Lakeit rattle off the list of relatives who grow or grew grapes in the area—starting when the most common variety was Concord—makes you think he might have grape juice running through his veins. Why did the family make the leap from grower to producer? It was partly because the price of grapes was declining and partly "because my little sister was always running back and forth when we were hauling grapes to Uncle Fred at Hernder Estates, and kept on saying 'Daddy, why don't we have a winery, why don't we have a winery?' And that got my dad's gears in motion. He figured this was a good way to set up his kids for life so we wouldn't need to work for someone else."

Caroline Cellars wines are 100 percent estate-grown. The vineyard at the winery comprises 26 acres (10 hectares) and they have another 15-acre (six-hectare) vineyard about half a kilometre away. They have a wide range of varieties, both vinifera and hybrids like Baco Noir, Maréchal Foch, and Vidal.

Pillitteri Estates Winery

Charles Pillitteri, vice-president of Pillitteri Estates Winery, has the brisk, efficient style of the shaker and mover. He's always on the go, and rattles out statistics, descriptions, opinions, and aspirations at machine-gun speed. His conversation is sprinkled with superlatives. "Pillitteri is the largest estate producer of icewine in the world." "The space given over for tastings is the largest permitted by Ontario's licensing authorities." "The concrete table in the barrel room is the longest in the world," and it's in "the largest single barrel room in Niagara."

There are many agendas at work here, and all the superlatives start to make sense. First, there's the icewine production. Pillitteri has long appreciated that, although icewine was something Niagara could do uniquely well, the domestic demand for it was limited. They quickly realized that the largest potential markets lay in Asia, and they have successfully cultivated them.

Charles Pillitteri visits Asia regularly and spends up to 200 days a year in Japan, China, Taiwan, Korea, Singapore, Indonesia, the Philippines, and Malaysia. He predicts a good future for icewine there, as well as in the United States, which, he says, is a market that's yet to be exploited.

Buoyant Asian sales have meant increasing production of icewine, and during the winter harvest Pillitteri uses ten presses to squeeze the sweet, viscous nectar out of 500 tonnes of grapes. Pillitteri now makes 35,000 cases (of 375-mL bottles) a year, about eight percent of Niagara's total, and it represents half the winery's case production of all wines. Selling icewine isn't without its problems. Vast amounts of counterfeit icewine are sold in Asia, and Charles Pillitteri works with the VQA and Wine Council of Ontario's initiatives to stamp

CLEANING THE EQUIPMENT

SHRIVELLING GRAPES CONCENTRATE SUGAR

it out. "Imitation is the highest form of flattery," he observes, "but we have to protect our product."

The maximum space given over to tourist tastings at the winery retail store is directly linked to the icewine sales in Asia. During the summer season, 12 to 20 buses a day pull into the winery, each carrying tourists from Asia. The store receives 80,000 to 100,000 visitors a year, two-fifths of them from Asian countries that are Pillitteri's markets. Sensitive to ethnic distinctions, Pillitteri Estates has built three separate tasting rooms, one each for Japanese, Chinese, and Korean visitors, and each in an appropriate style. Cultural awareness extends to labelling, too. In Chinese culture, gold and red are considered lucky, while in Japan it's blue and gold. For Chinese people, the number four is unlucky, the number eight lucky. Each of Pillitteri's icewine labels is designed for the wine's market destination, and each is printed in the appropriate language.

Coexisting with this Asian export dimension is a keen awareness of the Pillitteri family's Italian roots. The winery's founder, Gary Pillitteri, came to Canada from Sicily in 1948, and bought some of the 53 acres (21 hectares) that are now part of the winery's estate. Gradually he replaced the existing fruit trees with grapevines, and for many years sold his grapes to wineries—not all of it, though, for he was also a keen amateur winemaker. As it turned out, he was also a very good one, and he won a gold medal in an amateur wine competition in 1988 for his icewine. Encouraged by his success, he opened his own winery in 1993, and icewine became central to the business.

Gary Pillitteri was a man of more than one big ambition. The year he opened his winery, he was elected to the House of Commons as Liberal MP for Niagara Falls. He remained in the House of Commons until 2004, when he returned to the winery as its president. He's now actively involved in the business, along with son Charles, daughters Lucy (vice-president of marketing) and Connie (vice-president of operations), and son-in-law Jamie Slingerland, who manages the vineyards. Gary Pillitteri can be seen doing all manner of tasks. In the spring of 2005, the president and founder of the winery was building a wall to conceal the recyclable material from the store until it was collected. "You see what I'm relegated to now?" he laughed.

If icewine is a core Pillitteri flagship wine, it's by no means all the winery makes. There's a full range of whites and reds, including Vidal, Riesling, red Bordeaux blends, Cabernet Sauvignon, Merlot, and a number of late-harvest and select late-harvest dessert wines. The winemaker responsible for the wines is Sue-Ann Staff, who comes from a long line of Niagara grape growers. Staff studied at the University of Guelph and at Australia's famed Roseworthy College before joining Pillitteri in 1997. Since then, her wines have won a slew of awards (you can see them displayed in Pillitteri's reception area), and in 2002 she was named Ontario Winemaker of the Year. Among her recent successes are Riesling icewines, classics with perfectly poised fruit and acidity, and the reserve Merlots, which are complex, full bodied and full fruit. (Sadly, the Merlot vines are no longer with us, having succumbed to the harsh 2002-03 winter.)

Which takes us to the cellar, where many of the wines are aged. At 7,200 square feet (670 square metres), it's the largest single such room in the region. It can hold 1,500 barrels and contains about 400 at present. In the centre of the vaulted room is a 500-inch-long (12.9-metre) poured concrete table, with 23 chairs. Why 23? Because, Charles Pillitteri explains, it's a number with family significance. His father arrived in Canada on November 23, 1948; his mother was born on December 23; his sister Connie, on September 23; and his middle sister, Lucy, on February 23. He was born on August 2, but he was the third child, which gives a 2 and a 3. It all makes sense in terms of the Pillitteris' emphasis on family. Their labels depict a *carretto*, a Sicilian cart, a reminder of their roots. Here's a winery firmly focused on its family background, looking outward to commercial opportunities.

Hillebrand Estates Winery

Hillebrand Estates, a sibling winery to Peller Estates, has gone through several incarnations. It was founded by Joseph Pohorly (now owner of Joseph's Estate Wines), who called it Newark, after the original name of Niagara-on-the-Lake. It was renamed Hillebrand in 1982 after the German wine and spirits company, Scholl & Hillebrand, bought it. The company wasn't convinced that Newark was a recognized name and, because it planned to make wines in a German style, it wanted the winery to have a German identity. They started with one of Ontario's earliest icewines in 1983, and labelled it with the German name, Eiswein.

The German strategy was soon abandoned. In 1987 a French winemaker, Benoit Huchin, was hired, and within a few years Hillebrand was making more mainstream styles from Chardonnay and the Bordeaux varieties. Huchin's enduring achievement was the creation of Trius, initially named for the three varieties (Cabernet Sauvignon, Cabernet Franc, and Merlot). Trius Red was a well-priced, well-made blend that captured a niche in the

premium wine market and won numerous awards through the 1990s. It continues to be the Hillebrand line that's awarded most of the company's medals.

In 1994, the winery was purchased by Andrés, and Jean-Laurent Groux (who had been at Andrés for five years) became winemaker. For the next 15

WINERY DIRECTIONS

years, Groux raised the bar with Hillebrand wines and developed not only single-vineyard wines but also single-barrel wines. There are seven different single-barrel Chardonnays, each limited to 25 cases and each reflecting a different combination of vineyard and cooperage.

The vineyard- and barrel-designated wines appear in Hillebrand's Showcase Collection and are made as opportunities present themselves. During each vintage, the winemaker may identify a particular lot or barrel as having qualities that stand out from the rest, and the Showcase program enables them to bottle these small lots separately, rather than lose their distinctiveness in a blend of lots and barrels.

Hillebrand has 83 acres (33 hectares) of vineyards but draws on two others owned by private growers. The Glenlake Vineyard (actually four vineyards) is located near Lake Ontario and contributes to Trius wines, as well as single-vineyard wines in Hillebrand's Showcase line. The Huebel Vineyard near Queenston is Niagara's "first" vineyard—not in a historical sense, but because it's the first to start growth in the spring, first to flower in the summer, and the first to harvest in the fall.

The reason is that it's farther from Lake Ontario's moderating influences than any other vineyards below the Escarpment. In addition, by the time the summer winds reach the Huebel vineyard, they have travelled longer distances over land, warming up as they do so. Huebel has contributed a number of elegantly ripe wines to Hillebrand's single-vineyard and single-barrel releases. The Trius line also expanded from its original red to

include Chardonnay and a Trius Grand Red, and in 2005 three new single-variety Triuses were added: Merlot, Cabernet Franc, and Cabernet Sauvignon.

Hillebrand's present winemakers, Natalie Reynolds and Darryl Brooker, came to wine via different routes. Reynolds had a sports therapy clinic in Edmonton.She deepened her interest in wine through a tasting group, with friends in a sommelier course, and a friend who owned a premium wine boutique. She wanted to change careers and was thinking of doing a crush in Australia, New Zealand, or South Africa, but heard of Brock University's cool-climate wine program. She graduated from that "amazing course," doing some co-op placements in Niagara, and in August 2001 joined Hillebrand, where she was assistant winemaker to Jean-Laurent Groux until he left for Stratus Vineyards in 2004.

WINE-TOURING BY BICYCLE

Darryl Brooker was in the Australian navy and his connection with wine was through his wife, who comes from the Hunter Valley, one of Australia's premier wine regions. "Rather than spend time with the in-laws," he quips, "we used to go and visit the wineries." He says, "The navy trained people in lots of different occupations, but they didn't have much interest in wine," but he'd scoot off to wineries located near ports his ship docked in. "You could say the navy supported my wine studies." In 1997 Brooker enrolled in the wine science program at Charles Sturt University, then worked in the Barossa Valley, South Australia, and in New Zealand before joining Flat Rock Cellars in 2003 and Hillebrand in 2005.

Brooker and Reynolds work together on all the wines at Hillebrand, but they have their individual interests. Reynolds has more experience making sparkling wines, while Brooker's career has given him more background in Pinot Noir. They work on their own projects, Reynolds says. "If Darryl wants to try a natural ferment and I want to try out some different yeasts, there'll be different things going on."

They're identifying specific blocks in the vineyard for use in specific wines, like Trius Grand Red. "It makes no sense to treat all vineyards the same if some grapes are going to be used for a $12 red and others for a $40 red," Brooker says. They're also making Hillebrand wines with more of a fruit core. Both agree that Hillebrand wines are high quality, but many at the higher end were made for aging. They want to make them more approachable younger, and they want consumers to understand that an early-drinking wine isn't necessarily inferior to an age-worthy one. "It can still be intense and well-structured with more fruit core," Brooker says, "and that's what we're doing."

Both Reynolds and Brooker are keen on working with Pinot Noir, and aim to make it in a traditional Burgundy style—"like a Pinot Noir, not a Bordeaux red," Brooker says. They agree that it's a tricky grape and does best on the Beamsville Bench. But Natalie Reynolds adds, "You have to have a lot of love for the grape to give it all the attention it needs."

A FALL BUNCH

Domaine Vagners Winery

Closer to Lake Ontario, Martin Vagners owns the smallest commercial winery in Niagara: Domaine Vagners, which produces up to 100 cases of wine a year from six acres (2.5 hectares) of vines, and sells grapes to other wineries. Vagners began planting vines, mostly Bordeaux varieties, in 1990, and harvested his first crop in 1993. His first production was 100 cases of Cabernet Franc, and since then he has expanded his portfolio to include Merlot, a Bordeaux blend, Riesling, and Pinot Noir. His flagship, first made in 1994, is Creek Road Red, which combines Merlot, Cabernet Franc, and Cabernet Sauvignon.

Vagners cheerily calls himself a "nickel and dime" winery compared to those around him. It's still a hobby while he works full time at a winery supply company, and for him 200 cases would be "a big deal." His vines were hit hard by recent cruel winters, and he had virtually no grapes in 2003, but the experience hasn't dented his entrepreneurial

133

HOSING DOWN THE EQUIPMENT

spirit. He has planted more Pinot Noir in recent years, because it has proved quite winter-hardy, and he has built a below-ground cellar for his barrels. He'll take winemaking more seriously when he retires, he says. "You've just got to find your niche."

Strewn Winery

Along Lakeshore Road, only half a kilometre from the water, Strewn occupies a contoured concrete block building that used to be a fruit cannery. Constructed in the 1930s, it's been completely renovated, inside and out. Although it pales in size against big new buildings like Tawse, Stratus, and Jackson-Triggs, Strewn is one of the region's most attractive winery buildings. It has wine-making facilities and retail and tasting space,

plus a popular Provençal-themed bistro (Terroir La Cachette) and a cooking school. The Wine Country Cooking School is run by Jane Langdon, wife of winemaker Joe Will.

Will had been an amateur winemaker since his high school days and after a career in public relations in Calgary, decided in 1989 to try to make a living in wine. He moved to the Okanagan Valley and worked for a year at the Hainle winery, but decided he needed systematic training. In 1991, he went to Australia's famous wine school, Roseworthy College, graduated, and did a vintage at the Yalumba winery in the Barossa Valley.

When he returned to Canada he visited Niagara and met the Pillitteris, who were about to start their own winery. "Gary Pillitteri told me, 'You know, it's a family business, and you'll never have a chance to own any of it.' I said, 'That's okay, because in a few years I'm going to start a winery of my own.'" He made wine at Pillitteri while he and Jane Langdon planned their own winery. As they proceeded, Newman Smith, who had run Andrés for a number of years, became their business advisor. The first two vintages of the Strewn label, 1994 and 1995, were made at Pillitteri Estates while the cannery was being renovated and turned into a winery. The Strewn winery opened in 1997, and Smith joined as a partner.

The location was chosen as much with an eye to selling wine as growing grapes. With wholesale pricing through the LCBO, Will says, it makes more economic sense to sell as much as you can through the winery. The Niagara Canning Company, which was being used as a warehouse, didn't look that appealing, but it had plenty of space and is located on a road that's well-travelled in the tourist season. They purchased it in 1996. Influenced by a trip to California, Joe Will and Jane Langdon opted for a winery with a modern look with lots of light. They realized that the wine business was also about tourism, so they decided to incorporate a cooking school and restaurant. Rather than take on a restaurant themselves, though, they leased space, and the arrangement works well.

The name Strewn came up during a discussion between Will and Langdon. They decided they wanted a short name, one that had a strong sound, one that wasn't anyone's last name, and one that had no powerful connotations, so that they could put their own meaning on it. "Like . . . strewn," Will suggested, and the word stuck. "It means 'scattered,'" Will laughs, "and if you look at my desk, you'll see how it fits."

Strewn has 26 acres (10 hectares) of vines in two locations. Typically they grow a third of their own grapes and buy the rest from growers within 10 kilometres, making them firmly a Niagara-on-the-Lake winery. Their own vines are the classic varieties well known to consumers, like Chardonnay, Riesling, Pinot Blanc, Sauvignon Blanc, Merlot, and Cabernet Sauvignon. The only hybrid is Vidal, used for icewine and select late-harvest styles.

Will acknowledges that there are cool years when some varieties, like Cabernet Sauvignon, don't ripen. But, he points out, "regions that are on the fringe of grape-growing are the ones that have produced the most outstanding wines over time." Like many Niagara winemakers, he thinks that Riesling is the region's great underrated grape. "We have a good climate for it. Nearly everyone makes good Rieslings here, and they're often really very good. When you taste them with Rieslings from other parts of the world, our Rieslings are top drawer. But it has yet to receive the same level of recognition in the marketplace that Chardonnay has."

Newman Smith observes that Riesling sales are especially poor in the Toronto area. They're good from Hamilton to Niagara, which he attributes to people being in the area where they can taste and enjoy it. Joe Will adds that Chardonnay and Gewürztraminer also do well in the region. His location near the lake, where it's a little cooler in summer and warmer in winter, is particularly good for Gewürztraminer.

For all that, Strewn is probably best known for its big reds made from the three main Bordeaux grapes, Merlot, and the two Cabernets. The flagship wine is Strewn Three, a blend of those varieties, but it's made only in years when the fruit is judged good enough. In all, Strewn makes 17,000 cases a year and plans to grow to 30,000 cases.

Konzelmann Estate Winery

The beginnings of the Konzelmann winery sound familiar. Friedrich Konzelmann was a restaurateur who was interested in wine and started making his own at home. He was very successful and decided to go commercial, so he bought land, planted vines, and opened a winery. It's the short version of the story behind many Ontario wineries. The difference is that Konzelmann's story didn't take place in Ontario in the 1990s, but in Germany a hundred years earlier. Friedrich Konzelmann was the great-grandfather of Herbert Konzelmann, who opened Konzelmann Estate Winery in Niagara in 1988. In 1893, Friedrich had opened the first Konzelmann winery near Stuttgart. Within a few years his production was about 22,000 cases.

Fast forward to 1958, to his great-grandson, Herbert, who had graduated from the Weinsberg

Institute, Germany's oldest viticulture and oenology school, and was starting work in the family winery. By then, production had increased to about 40,000 cases. But Germany was rebuilding, and by the 1970s, the city of Stuttgart was encroaching on agricultural and viticultural lands, and land prices were rising. Herbert Konzelmann looked to Canada, and in 1984 bought 85 acres (34 hectares) of land near

MIXED FARM

the shore of Lake Ontario. He planted 30,000 vines and opened his winery in 1986. In 2000 Matthias Boss joined the winery and now shares winemaking with Herbert Konzelmann. He's a graduate of the same oenology school at Weinsberg and worked in Germany's Pfalz region and in Saint Emilion, Bordeaux, before coming to Niagara.

Konzelmann pioneered vertical vine training, which results in higher vines. This exposes the fruit to more sun and wind, reduces their moisture content, and increases their sugar and fruit intensity. His emphasis was on Riesling varieties, and he now produces four different styles of Riesling table wine, Riesling icewine, and a sparkling Riesling made by the Charmat method. A new sparkling wine, made from Chardonnay, Pinot Noir, and Riesling in the

méthode champenoise, is being released in late 2006. The winery's total production is about 40,000 cases a year.

The premium tier at Konzelmann Estate is the Winemaker's Collection, made from the oldest vines in the vineyard. The grapes are thinned three times during the growing season and are hand picked. Varietals and blends in this line are all distinguished by fruit purity and good varietal character, and they include Chardonnay, Riesling, Pinot Grigio, Merlot, Pinot Noir, and a Cabernet-Merlot blend.

Konzelmann Estate is expanding its facilities in 2006. On the sales side, there will be a bigger retail store and an observation tower from which visitors can look over the vineyards and lake, north to Toronto. At the production end, Matthias Boss points out that the new temperature-controlled underground barrel room will allow him to increase production of the Winemaster's Collection wines.

Palatine Hills Estate Winery

Palatine Hills Estate Winery opened in 2003, partly as a result of an unexpected success. Owners John and Barbara Neufeld had been growing grapes and providing juice to wineries in Ontario, Pennsylvania, and New York since the mid-1990s. But in the plush 1998 Niagara vintage, they found themselves with more Vidal icewine juice than they could sell, so they enlisted the help of a local winemaker to vinify it. Two years later, when they and a winery failed to agree on a price for his icewine must, they made their own wine again. The following year, the excellent 2001 vintage, the Neufelds made not only icewine but also some table wines and some late-harvest styles.

But what really persuaded them to graduate from grape growers to winery owners was the critical acclaim of their first vintage. They entered the 1998 icewine in a competition, and it was named Ontario Wine of the Year for 2003. With demand for their wine growing, the Neufelds went into business the same year, naming the winery after a nearby location identified on an old map of the area as Palatine Hills.

They now produce 5,000 cases of wine a year, in addition to icewine, from a 120-acre (48-hectare)

NETTED VINES

vineyard planted completely in vinifera except for Vidal, which is dedicated to the icewine. A vineyard that size produces far more than 5,000 cases of wine, of course, and Neufeld sells grapes and juice to other wineries and also supplies juice for the home winemaking market. He tells amateurs that they can make their wine "from the same grapes and juices the professionals use," and the winery provides winemaking facilities and guidance for customers who don't want to make wine at home.

Since 2001 Palatine Hills has been a working partnership of John Neufeld, who grows the grapes, and David Hojnoski, who came on board to makes the wines in 2002. Each collaborates in the other's sphere.

Stonechurch Vineyards

Stonechurch Vineyards lies midway between Palatine Hills and the Welland Canal. There's so little light pollution at Stonechurch's site that for years people used to come to the winery, sip the wine, and get a good view of the night sky. The vines they sat among belong to one of the largest family-owned vineyards in Niagara. Stonechurch has 200 acres (80 hectares) under vines in five separate locations, most near the shore of Lake Ontario. Vinifera varieties were first planted in 1972 by Lambert and Grace Hunse, who emigrated from the Netherlands in the 1950s. Their son, Rick, and his wife, Fran, opened the winery in 1990, and named it after a nearby church that dates back to the 1850s. The main varieties planted are Sauvignon Blanc, Gewürztraminer, Riesling, and Chardonnay, for the whites, and Cabernet Sauvignon, Pinot Noir, Cabernet Franc, and some young Syrah vines for the reds.

Rick Hunse, who ran Stonechurch until his death in 2005, had his sights set high. In 2004, he brought on board as winemaker Terence van Rooyen, who had been at Cilento Wines. Van Rooyen brought experience from his native South Africa, where he had made wine at the KWV. In addition to van Rooyen, Stonechurch acquired one of Cilento's Niagara vineyards. "So I came with a vineyard," van Rooyen quips. It meant, of course, that he was very familiar with some of the grapes he'd work with, because he'd made Pinot Noir, Sauvignon Blanc, and Riesling sparkling wine from them.

Hunse planned to increase Stonechurch's current production of 25,000 cases. In 2004 he renewed the winery's barrel inventory, buying 100 new French and American barrels for Chardonnay, Pinot Noir, Cabernet Franc, and Cabernet Sauvignon. The renewal continued with a new president, John Geci, whose varied background includes education, the grocery industry, and the military. A wine lover with a special passion for Pinot Noir, Geci says, "I always promoted excellence in education, and I do the same for wine." He plans to focus on a few key varieties like Cabernet Sauvignon, Sauvignon Blanc, and Riesling, and he'd like to see more people drinking Gewürztraminer. "I don't know if it's the name or what, but it's not as popular as it should be."

Van Rooyen produced several very good wines in 2004, his first vintage at Stonechurch. The Sauvignon Blanc is crisp and fruit-driven, and the Gewürztraminer has solid tropical fruit and spicy flavours. There's an interesting Morio Muscat with floral, tropical, and lychee flavours. (Stonechurch is one of two or three wineries with this variety.) And if you're looking for an older wine, a glance through the shelves at Stonechurch will turn up older Cabernet Franc and Cabernet Sauvignon, not to mention icewines from the early and mid-1990s.

OPPOSITE: **VINES ON THE LAKESHORE**

PAGES 142–43: **THE COLOURS OF THE VINE**

WINE MATURING IN BARRELS

THE WINERIES

Caroline Cellars Winery
1028 Line 2
Niagara-on-the-Lake, ON L0S 1J0
Tel: 905-468-8814
www.lakeitfarms.com

Château des Charmes
1025 York Road
Niagara-on-the-Lake, ON L0S 1P0
Tel: 905-262-4219
www.chateaudescharmes.com

Coyote's Run Estate Winery
Concession 5 Road
St. David's, ON L0S 1P0
Tel: 905-682-8310
www.coyotesrunwinery.com

Domaine Vagners Winery
1973 Four Mile Creek Road
Niagara-on-the-Lake, ON L0S 1J0
Tel: 905-468-7296

Frogpond Farm
1385 Larkin Road
Niagara-on-the-Lake, ON L0S 1J0
Tel: 905-468-1079
www.frogpondfarm.ca

Hillebrand Estates Winery
1249 Niagara Stone Road
Niagara-on-the-Lake, ON L0S 1J0
Tel: 905-468-7123
www.hillebrand.com

Inniskillin
Niagara Parkway at Line 3
Niagara-on-the-Lake, ON L0S 1J0
Tel: 905-468-2178
www.inniskillin.com

Jackson-Triggs Niagara Estate Winery
2145 Niagara Stone Road
Niagara-on-the-Lake, ON L0S 1J0
Tel: 905-468-4637
www.jacksontriggswinery.com

Joseph's Estate Wines
1811 Niagara Stone Road
Niagara-on-the-Lake, ON L0S 1J0
Tel: 905-468-1259
www.josephsestatewines.com

Konzelmann Estate Winery
1096 Lakeshore Road
Niagara-on-the-Lake, ON L0S 1J0
Tel: 905-935-2866
www.konzelmannwines.com

Lailey Vineyard
15940 Niagara Parkway
Niagara-on-the-Lake, ON L0S 1J0
Tel: 905-468-0503
www.laileyvineyard.com

Maleta Estate Winery
450 Queenston Road
Niagara-on-the-Lake, ON L0S 1J0
Tel: 905-685-8486
www.maletawinery.com

Marynissen Estates
RR #6, Concession 1
Niagara-on-the-Lake, ON L0S 1J0
Tel: 905-468-7270
www.marynissen.com

Niagara College Teaching Winery
135 Taylor Road
Niagara-on-the-Lake, ON L0S 1J0
Tel: 905-641-2252
www.nctwinery.ca

THE WINERIES

Palatine Hills Estate Winery
911 Lakeshore Road
Niagara-on-the-Lake, ON L0S 1J0
Tel: 905-646-9617
www.palatinehillsestatewinery.com

Peller Estates
290 John Street East
Niagara-on-the-Lake, ON L0S 1J0
Tel: 905-468-4678
www.peller.com

Pillitteri Estates Winery
1696 Niagara Stone Road
Niagara-on-the-Lake, ON L0S 1J0
Tel: 905-468-3147
www.pillitteri.com

Reif Estate Winery
15608 Niagara Parkway
Niagara-on-the-Lake, ON L0S 1J0
Tel: 905-468-7738
www.reifwinery.com

Riverview Cellars Estate Winery
15376 Niagara Parkway
Niagara-on-the-Lake, ON L0S 1J0
Tel: 905-262-0636
www.riverviewcellars.com

Stonechurch Vineyards
1242 Irvine Road
Niagara-on-the-Lake, ON L0S 1J0
Tel: 905-935-3535
www.stonechurch.com

Stratus Vineyards
2059 Niagara Stone Road
Niagara-on-the-Lake, ON L0S 1J0
Tel: 905-468-1806
www.stratuswines.com

Strewn Winery
1339 Lakeshore Road
Niagara-on-the-Lake, ON L0S 1J0
Tel: 905-468-1229
www.strewnwinery.com

LAKE ERIE NORTH SHORE AND PELEE ISLAND

"EVERYONE KNOWS ABOUT NIAGARA PENINSULA, AND THERE'S ALL THIS
TALK ABOUT PRINCE EDWARD COUNTY, BUT LAKE ERIE NORTH SHORE IS A
PLACE THAT MAKES GREAT WINES, ESPECIALLY OUR REDS."

—CARLO NEGRI
COLIO ESTATE WINES

Lake Erie North Shore and Pelee Island are Ontario's second and third Designated Viticultural Areas in size. Pelee Island has no wineries these days, although it has Pelee Island Winery's 550 acres (220 hectares) of vineyards, and is well worth visiting. Lake Erie North Shore has a dozen wineries, and the region has established a reputation for making quality wines, especially reds. The two largest wineries make close to half of the VQA wine sold in the LCBO. Moreover, it's a dynamic region that's growing steadily in quality and in number of producers.

Still, it's difficult not to sympathize with winemaker Carlo Negri of Colio Estate Wines when he quietly observes, "Everyone knows about Niagara Peninsula, and there's all this talk about Prince Edward County, but Lake Erie North Shore is a place that makes great wines, especially our reds." Negri isn't a whiner. What he says is regrettably true: the southwest's wine regions are below the radar of most Ontario wine consumers.

The Lake Erie North Shore wine region lies, predictably, along the north shore of Lake Erie. It runs from the Detroit River in the west to Leamington, with another concentration of vineyards to the east, near Blenheim. Pelee Island lies 15 miles (25 kilometres) offshore. At this point, Canada is south of the nearest parts of the United States. In fact it's so far

OPPOSITE: **BETWEEN VINE AND BOTTLE**

south that parts of half the states in the continental United States lie to the *north* of Pelee Island.

These two regions are along the same latitudes as Tuscany and Rome, while Niagara is on line with the northerly regions of Bordeaux and Burgundy. Lake Erie North Shore gets more sunshine hours than anywhere else in Canada. Couple that with the warm waters of Lake Erie, the shallowest of the Great Lakes, and you have a growing season that's ideal for viticulture. The effect is enhanced by the fact that vineyards on Lake Erie North Shore are generally planted on gentle slopes that face south and southeast, giving them long exposure to sun during the growing season.

The season is even longer on Pelee Island. It's the southernmost part of Canada, with as many heat units as California's Napa Valley It has a growing season that's up to 30 days longer than on the mainland, and grapes are often harvested at the end of August. Even grapes intended for late-harvest style wines are picked much earlier than elsewhere, often by mid-October.

These regions aren't as dry as many comparably warm wine regions in other parts of the world, though, and two-thirds of the North Shore's and Pelee Island's precipitation falls during the growing season, which can make the regions' vines more vulnerable to mildew. In addition, much of the precipitation is generated by storms that follow a regular track across the region, and hail damage is another threat to vines. Moreover, winters are much colder than in other warm-climate wine regions. Temperatures here can drop well below –4°F (–20°C) and, like Niagara Peninsula's, Lake Erie North Shore's vineyards suffered serious winter damage in recent years, especially during the winters of 2002–03 and 2004–05. Some vineyards are sprouting wind machines among the vinifera vines, so as to lessen the effects of the cold. As for soils, they're mainly fertile clay, which holds the water from the melting winter snow well enough to give the vines a good start in the spring.

The longer and warmer growing season has encouraged the planting of red Bordeaux varieties. A number of the regions' most impressive wines are blends, as well as varietal Cabernet Sauvignons and Cabernet Francs. In addition there are excellent Chardonnays, Rieslings, and some very interesting wines made from Baco Noir and Maréchal Foch. But there's a prevailing sense that the more highly valued vinifera-based wines will cement the reputation of these southwestern Ontario regions.

Viticulture and winemaking began here in the 1860s, but although there were perhaps two dozen wineries by 1900, the local market couldn't support them. Many closed when tobacco was planted in the region, although there was a short-lived resurgence during Prohibition (1916–1927) when wine was exempted from the ban imposed on sales of beer and distilled spirits. The two regions took part in the renaissance of Ontario's wine industry from the 1970s, when new wineries began to plant vinifera varieties. Investors began to take an interest in southwestern Ontario when Niagara land prices began to rise in the later 1970s. Several vineyards were planted at that time and in 1981, two of the regions' biggest wineries opened: Colio Estate Winery in Harrow, with vineyards on the shore of Lake Erie, and Pelee Island Winery, which has vineyards on the island. Since then, the number of wineries has steadily increased.

THE WINERIES OF LAKE ERIE NORTH SHORE

D'Angelo Estate Winery

One of the phenomena that accompanied the globalization of the wine industry was the "flying winemakers"—men and women who follow the seasons and make wine each year in two, sometimes more, parts of the world, usually in different hemispheres. Australian winemakers might make wine in Australia in April and in California in September, while French winemakers might head for Chile during their own spring.

Canada's flying winemaker is Salvatore D'Angelo, but he's a flying winemaker with a difference in that he travels east–west, between Lake Erie North Shore and British Columbia's Okanagan Valley. Sal D'Angelo, as everyone knows him, made Canadian wine history by being the first individual

to own wineries in Ontario and British Columbia. Vincor owns wineries in both provinces (Inniskillin and Jackson-Triggs have Niagara and Okanagan brands) but D'Angelo is the first private owner to do so. In 2001, he bought land on the Naramata Bench of the Okanagan Valley and built a winery and bed and breakfast, and in 2005 he produced his first vintage. In Lake Erie North Shore, he runs one of the older wineries: it opened in 1989 to produce wine from vines he began planting in 1983.

D'Angelo is a former schoolteacher who learned winemaking from his father and spent time learning vine management from his grandfather in Italy. He started looking for a vineyard in 1979 and bought a farm east of Amherstburg, about five miles (eight kilometres) from Lake Erie. There he planted 42 acres (17 hectares) in Vidal, Maréchal Foch, Baco Noir, Cabernet Franc, Chambourcin, Pinot Noir, and Chardonnay. At first, the vineyard proved suit-

SHADED OUTDOOR GARDENS AND A CAFÉ ACCOMMODATE BUS LOADS OF TOURISTS

able for hybrids but too cold in winter for vinifera, so D'Angelo later bought land on the lakeshore near Colchester for vinifera. He sold it to the new Viewpointe winery in 2001 to raise money for his Okanagan venture. Now, working with the original vineyard, he has made it more vinifera-friendly by installing a wind machine. John Klassen, the vineyard manager, says it has really reduced winter damage.

Persistence and success with his vineyards earned D'Angelo the 1999 Grape King award—the first time, since it started in 1956, that the title had gone to a grape grower outside Niagara Peninsula. His achievement was all the more impressive because during much of the 1990s he'd suffered from Guillain-Barré Syndrome, and effectively lost the use of his legs for more than three years.

PRUNED VINES

D'Angelo Estate winery produces about 5,000 cases of wine a year, including some impressive wines made from hybrids. The little-known Chambourcin makes a complex, quite intense red in D'Angelo's hands, and the Old Vines Foch has layers of flavours and accents. The Pinot Noirs from warm vintages like 2002 are huge, dense reds with full tannic grip. Overall, D'Angelo's wines show their vintages very well, with concentrated fruit in 1999 and 2002 and lighter styles in 2004. It's an effect that consumers can try for themselves, because D'Angelo sells many older vintages of whites and reds that go back to the early and mid-1990s.

Sanson Estate Winery

Chef Dennis Sanson traces his winemaker lineage to a long interest in food and farming. He grew up near Kent County and worked on farms there, developed a love of food, and graduated from the culinary program at Windsor's St. Clair College in 1980. Wine was going through a transition in Ontario during the 1980s, and he started making it as a hobby. Then, he says with his dry humour, "the hobby got out of hand." A self-confessed "closet farmer," he bought a 100-acre (40-hectare) lot and thought about planting vines. It didn't seem the best spot for grapes, he readily admits, but the soil was similar to that at Niagara's Henry of Pelham, so Sanson planted Baco Noir, one of Henry of Pelham's specialties.

Now he has seven acres (three hectares) planted equally in Baco Noir and Vidal. He also buys Chardonnay, Sauvignon Blanc, Merlot, Cabernet Sauvignon, Cabernet Franc, and Shiraz from growers in Essex and Kent County. He produced his first vintage in 2000 and opened the winery the next year. His current production is about 4,000 cases, and he aims eventually to make between 10,000 and 12,000 cases a year. As well as grapes, Sanson grows heirloom vegetables, and at the right time of year you can buy peppers, squash, and eggplant in many different sizes, shapes, and colours in his wine shop. He has started making cheese, and from the winery you can catch sight of his herd of Limousin cattle. "We grow wine and steaks," he quips.

Sanson Estate wines span the range from a racy Sauvignon Blanc to big, portlike reserve Baco Noirs (like the 2002 vintage) that are silky-textured and chock full of plum, prune, and chocolate flavours. He's modest about the Baco, and says, "You'd have to be a fool to make a bad wine from 2002." His Vidal icewine has higher acidity than most, making it food-friendly. Sanson says he used to be uncertain about icewine, but he likes his own because of the acidity. There's also a red blend called Bird Dog, which sounds a bit like Bordeaux. The blend does, too, with Cabernet Franc, Cabernet Sauvignon, and Merlot, but there's also 20 percent Zweigelt. It makes for a medium-bodied, flavoursome red. "When I first bottled it, I hated it," Sanson says, "but I let it sit a year in the bottle and now it's great."

For Dennis Sanson, viticulture is an integral part of his environment. He has 35 acres (14 hectares) of woodland and wetland, and is actively regenerating them. He has added three areas of wetland and planted thousands of trees on his property. But then, as he talks seriously about his land, he can't help joking: "This is the most haunted winery in Ontario, too. We're right by an old cemetery that goes back to the 1840s. We have wines and spirits."

Muscedere Vineyards

At Muscedere Vineyards, brothers Fabio and Roberto Muscedere planted 12 acres (five hectares) of vines in 2003 and opened their winery in 2006. They're focusing on classic reds (Pinot Noir, Merlot, Cabernet Franc, Cabernet Sauvignon, Malbec, and Syrah), along with Chardonnay, Riesling, Pinot Grigio, and Sauvignon Blanc. Their vineyard is north of Harrow, five miles (eight kilometres) from the cooling effects of the lake, and they expect these growing conditions, together with the clay soil of their site, to give them small, intensely-flavoured grapes that will make big red wines.

Sons of Italian immigrants, the Muscedere brothers (Roberto is an engineer, Fabio is in marketing) visited family in Italy every other year and spent time in their grandfather's vineyard in Lazio. "We grew up around wine," Roberto says. "It was on our table, being Italian, and allowed us to develop a curiosity about wine. We thought about having a family vineyard, and then, about four or five years ago, we started to look at our own back yard and saw the great wines. So we're combining our Italian heritage and the New World we live in." Their first vintage, 2004, gave them 300 cases of Chardonnay, Riesling, and Cabernet Franc, and in 2005 they made 1,000 cases of wine from their own vines and grapes bought from other growers. They're aiming at making 10,000 cases.

VINES ON THE LAKESHORE

NIAGARA'S NATURAL STONE IS PART OF EVERYDAY LIFE

Sprucewood Shores Estate Winery

Sprucewood Shores Estate is a winery-in-the-making. Gordon Mitchell, who was raised on a farm but worked as an auto plant manager, chose a 35-acre (14-hectare) site behind a row of cottages on the lakeshore near Harrow. He figured that vines there would benefit from the offshore breeze, and he says his hunch has borne fruit. He also liked the soil there, which has more clay than the sandy soil often found along the edge of Lake Erie. Starting in 1990, Mitchell planted eight varieties: Chardonnay, Vidal, Pinot Gris, and Riesling for whites, and Pinot Noir, Gamay, Merlot, Cabernet Franc, and Cabernet Sauvignon for reds.

He has been selling his grapes to local wineries for several years, but in 2004 made his first vintage,

a few hundred cases of red wine from the Bordeaux varieties. Gordon Mitchell's daughter, Tanya, made the wine with the assistance of some local wine makers. She's a chemical engineer by training, but did some amateur winemaking and has worked at wineries in Australia and Lake Erie North Shore. Once he has an inventory, Gordon Mitchell will open his winery in 2006 or 2007.

Erie Shore Vineyard

Erie Shore Vineyard is a small winery whose owners have no real wish to see it grow too much. Harvey and Alma Hollingshead produce 2,000 to 3,000 cases of wine a year and can see doubling that, but no more. "For us," Harvey says, "this is a second career, and we tackle it from the angle of what we want to do, not what we could do." He'd worked in banking and she had a degree in crop science. They bought a 40-acre (16-hectare) uncultivated plot of land near Lake Erie in 1994, and planted grapes in 1997. Now they have 15 acres (six hectares) planted in vines and another eight acres (three hectares) ready to go.

The vines represent seven varieties, four vinifera (Riesling, Chardonnay, Cabernet Franc, and Zweigelt) and three hybrids (Vidal, Chambourcin, and Baco Noir). Harvey is bullish about hybrids and deplores the prejudice against them. He and Alma considered Merlot, he says, but they preferred Zweigelt as a blending grape with Cabernet Franc and found it better suited to their site. They make a small range of affordable table wines using only their own grapes. Included are a crisp, fruity Riesling, a beautiful salmon-bronze dry rosé made from Cabernet Franc, called Summer Sun, and a two-thirds Cabernet Franc and one-third Zweigelt blend called Duet, which is fruity, spicy, and complex. At the sweeter end of the spectrum, there's a late-harvest and an icewine, both made from Vidal.

Erie Shore also makes a Cabernet Franc that includes 15 percent Baco Noir. The blend was an accident, Harvey says. One evening he wanted a bottle of wine for dinner and grabbed two opened bottles from the tasting room. One was a nearly full bottle of Cabernet Franc, the other a near empty bottle of Baco Noir. He poured the Baco into the Cabernet and found that it improved it.

This is a modest family operation in which Alma Hollingshead looks after the vines and Harvey makes the wines, but the lines aren't definitively drawn. On a summer day just after the grapes had turned colour, when flocks of birds were seen in the vineyard (they prefer Baco Noir), the Hollingshead children and friends were riding all-terrain vehicles along the rows to scare off the birds. The Hollingsheads stopped using bangers so as not to bother their neigbours, and they net many of the vines each year.

They're committed to greeting their visitors personally, using their own fruit, and making their wine on the farm. "I always tell my customers," Harvey Hollingshead says, "that the first time the grapes leave the farm is in the bottle that they buy."

VINES IN WINTER

Colchester Ridge Estate Winery

Nearby is the Colchester Ridge Estate Winery, owned by Bernard and Nancy Gorski. Bernard grew up on a farm ("I've been farming since I was eight years old," he says) and runs a trucking business that carries a lot of liquids, like wine and whisky, in tankers. He's been doing this since 1975, and during that time he followed the progress of Ontario wine, got to know a lot of the prominent people in the wine industry, and kept hearing the refrain, "if we could only get better grapes, we could make better wine." This resonated on the farmer within, and Gorski thought, "I can grow better grapes. It's easy."

He planted 12 acres (five hectares) of Cabernet Sauvignon, Merlot, Gewürztraminer, and Chardonnay in 2001, and took a first small harvest in 2004. The Colchester Ridge vineyard is set a couple of hundred yards from the lake and is 70 feet above its level, and a wind machine keeps winter temperatures high enough to prevent damage to the vines. In the 2004–05 winter, Bernard Gorski says, the lowest temperature in his vineyard was −2°F (−18°C), 10 degrees warmer than it was half a kilometre away.

In 2005, he produced about 900 cases of wine and plans to take production to 3,000 cases. Although he leaves open the possibility of buying grapes in the future, he says, "So far, I'm proud enough to say I'll use only my own." Gorski wants Colchester Ridge to become a high-end boutique winery, but admits that he can't tell what his vines are capable of until they're mature. In the meantime, he might not be building castles in the air, but he opens his winery in 2006, and has ambitious plans to erect a larger stone structure in the style of a château.

Viewpointe Estate Winery

Every self-respecting wine region has to have at least one showpiece winery, and for Lake Erie North Shore, it's Viewpointe Estate Winery. Open in 2006, the public buildings (angled toward the lake in a V-shape) are built right on the shore of Lake Erie. An Agriculture Building provides visitors with information on viticulture and winemaking. Visitors can also visit the underground aging cellar that accommodates 800 barrels. Unlike most cellars, where there's dim lighting and an atmosphere evoking age, Viewpointe's is brightly lit. There's a practical reason, says John Fancsy, one of Viewpointe Estate's owners: "It's so that we can see what to clean. I don't believe there's any room for mould in a barrel room." They'd have liked to build it into a hill, he adds, "But this is Essex County. There are no hills."

The other building on the Viewpointe site, the Hospitality Building, houses a culinary centre

VINEOUS DESIGN

on the ground floor and an underground tasting bar that adjoins the barrel room. Rooms for events and functions are on the second level, with panoramic views over the lake (and on clear days to Pelee Island) and back over the vineyards. The actual winemaking facility, however, is across the road. It's a utilitarian structure with all the equipment needed to make Viewpointe's quality wines.

The winery was started by John and Steve Fancsy and Steve's wife, Jean. The Fancsys were in the auto parts business (a key part of Windsor's economy) but they sold their interest to start the winery. Steve is involved in market gardening and now manages Viewpointe's vineyards, while John Fancsy makes the wine with assistant winemaker Jocelyn Clark.

They have a total of 50 acres (20 hectares) on three locations under vines, and grow mainly Cabernet Franc, Cabernet Sauvignon, Merlot, and Pinot Noir, along with Chardonnay, Riesling, Pinot Gris, and Sauvignon Blanc, and a little Gewürztraminer, Tempranillo, and Viognier. Their vineyards, planted from 1999 to 2001, are both on the lake and farther inland, so that they get different climatic influences. In warm, cloudy years, the vineyards near the lake accumulate more heat (especially the vines farthest from the shore. But during sunny years, the other vineyard accumulates more heat because the land has a slight south-facing slope. "It depends on the season," John Fancsy says. "One is better than the other, and we have both. I'd like to say it was planned, but it was luck."

Clearly, though, there's a lot of planning here. The Fancsys sized up the situation in Lake Erie North Shore before deciding to build their impressive winery (there are plans to add accommodation later). This area is within 60 miles (100 kilometres) of six million people in Canada and the United States, and it's their only wine region. "But if we want them to come to wineries, we have to give them a destination, somewhere to go, and this will be a destination." They're confident they can pull it off. John Fancsy observes wryly, "If you can handle the automotive business, you can handle anything."

END OF A ROW

Visitors will taste a good range of wines at Viewpointe, including Chardonnay made wholly from Lake Erie North Shore grapes and one of the all-vinifera wines made here. Production has been growing steadily: 2,500 cases in 2001; 4,000 in 2002; 6,000 in 2004; and 10,000 in 2005. (Like most Ontario wineries, Viewpointe was hit hard by the winter of 2002–03.)

The Fancsys also own a nursery in Lake County, California, and are experimenting with various clones and varieties. They're very impressed with their Cabernet Franc and plan to expand the Pinot Noir. "This is a great site for Pinot Noir," Fancsy says, "because it's so dry."

Why the name Viewpointe? Standing on the balcony of the second floor of the Hospitality Building, John Fancsy points up the coast. "We're close to Point Pelee and just look at the view. And besides, we always have to have an opinion, a point of view, on everything."

Colio Estate Wines

Carlo Negri, winemaker at Colio Estate Wines since it opened in 1980, was a bit skeptical when he was asked to join the company. He was working at the Collavini winery in Friuli, in northern Italy, at the time, and admits, "I didn't know they grew grapes in Canada. I knew they did in California . . ." But he came to this winery, founded by a group of Canadian and Italian investors who obtained the first winery licence in the region since Prohibition, and began to produce wine from hybrid varieties. They were bought from growers in southwest Ontario and the Niagara Peninsula until Colio purchased vineyards in 1990. The winery is now owned by one of the original shareholders—Enzo DeLuca, a Toronto entrepreneur—and Joe Berardo, a Portuguese businessman with a passion for wine.

In the 1980s, Negri says, "The market wanted 90 percent white wines, and I had red hybrids, so I started making white wine from red grapes." He made one wine called Bianco Secco from De Chaunac, Seyval Blanc, and other varieties. He gestures toward bottles of Colio's premium CEV Cabernet Sauvignon and Merlot and shakes his head. "At that time, we couldn't even dream of making the wines we make today." Those wines cover a wide range, including crisp, fruity Blanc de Noirs, sparkling wine made by the Charmat method from Pinot Noir, and fruit-driven, complex Pinot Grigio, Riesling, and Chardonnay. But you don't have to dig deep into Negri's wine soul to strike red. "If you really want a good wine with dinner, it's red," he says, before quickly adding, "White is good, too."

Negri's premium reds are consistently well made and well structured with pure fruit showing through. In the CEV series, the Cabernet Franc stands out for its typicity and quality, and it's a wine that will age 10 years or more. The highest tier at Colio, though, is Signature, and the 2002 Meritage (an equal blend of the Cabernets and Merlot) was released in late 2005. It's a beautifully made blend, with rich fruit, fine balance, and fine, ripe tannins that will cellar for many years. There are excellent late-harvest and icewines, too, with a fine acid spine that moderates the sweetness. Negri's skill across his portfolio has been recognized by his peers, and he was named Winemaker of the Year at the 2005 Ontario Wine Awards.

Colio now owns 200 acres (80 hectares) of vines close to the lake south of Harrow and buys additional grapes from local and Niagara growers. Colio

WORKING THE SOIL

OPPOSITE: **DURING HARVEST**

makes 200,000 cases of wine a year, about 60 percent VQA classified. Reds predominate in the VQA wines, and Negri is very positive about Cabernet Sauvignon, Cabernet Franc, and Merlot in particular: "They do well year after year in the longer growing season." The reds are barrel aged, but only small volumes of Chardonnay see any wood. "We found the market is better for un-oaked, most people prefer un-oaked," Negri says, "especially when the Chardonnay is good."

Colio is also expanding into the Niagara Peninsula. In 2005, the company bought a 20-acre (eight-hectare) vineyard near the Inniskillin winery, in Niagara-on-the-Lake. They'll eventually build a winery and be the first to produce wine in two of Ontario's designated viticultural areas. Another initiative that sets Colio off from other wineries is

THE START OF A CRUSH

a 2004 partnership with Jean-Michel Moueix, who owns several Bordeaux châteaux, notably Château La Tour du Pin Figeac in St. Emilion. Colio now represents Moueix's wines in Ontario, and Moueix represents Colio in Europe. The first shipment of Colio wines comprised Vidal and Cabernet Franc icewines. It will be interesting to watch the reception when Colio's Meritage, a Bordeaux blend, hits the shelves in Europe.

Pelee Island Winery

Pelee Island Winery is Lake Erie North Shore's largest by far, and it has established a position in both of the region's appellations. Grapes are grown on Pelee Island, picked early in the morning, around three or four o'clock, then taken by ferry (a 90-minute trip) to the winery on the lakeshore.

The winery was founded in 1982 by Austrian winemaker, Walter Strehn, whose family had a winery in Austria. Strehn knew that grapes had grown on Pelee Island in the past and bought up large tracts of inexpensive land. The winery now has 550 acres (220 hectares) of vines on the island, almost as much as the total plantings in the Lake Erie North Shore region.

The winemaker and president is genial, outgoing Walter Schmoranz, who came to the winery from Germany in 1986. He learned winemaking in Germany where, he says, "It's just another trade." He studied at the leading German wine schools, Geisenheim and Weinsberg, and worked as a winemaker and grape grower for a while before thinking it would be good to do a few years somewhere else. In 1986, he had offers from Ontario and Long Island, New York, but the Ontario winery got its paperwork organized first, so he opted for it. Having already had a vacation in British Columbia in 1982, he was looking forward to the mountains and was shocked when he landed on the dead-flat shores of Lake Erie.

He has now been with Pelee Island Winery more than 20 years. Schmoranz has seen it grow from a winery started in 1979 by "some butchers and bakers from Kitchener, who went out every week-end to have some fun" to one of Canada's biggest commercial wineries. Pelee Island winery makes 300,000 cases of wine a year, up to 80 percent of it VQA, depending on the vintage. Most of the grapes come from the Pelee Island vineyards, but some are purchased from growers in Lake Erie North Shore and Niagara Peninsula. Even so, this is the largest grape-growing winery in Ontario.

The main white varieties grown on the island are Chardonnay, Gewürztraminer, Riesling, Sauvignon Blanc, Viognier, Pinot Gris, and Seyval Blanc. There are many more reds and they include Pinot Noir, Cabernet Sauvignon, Cabernet Franc, and Merlot as well as Shiraz, Tempranillo, Gamay, Zweigelt, Baco Noir, and Chambourcin. Schmoranz is positive about the hybrids: "People talk down the hybrids, but it's a matter of finding blending partners. They have great potential."

The soil on the island is heavy clay on lime-stone, and it produces small berries with very concentrated flavours and pigmentation. Despite the fact that the island has a low elevation—parts in the centre actually lie below the level of the lake—the soil is well drained. The reason is that there's a subterranean system of dikes and drains that draws water away—and the flow can be reversed for irrigation, if necessary. The cli-mate favours red grapes. Pelee Island lies on the same latitude as Mendocino County in northern California, and the growing-season is long and warm. A constant wind across the island helps reduce moisture and mildew.

Grapevines were introduced, but Pelee Island's 10,000 acres (4,000 hectares) are home to tens of

SUN CASCADES IN THE WINERY ENTRANCE

thousands of species of birds, insects, plants, and trees, some of which find their way onto Pelee Island Winery labels. This is no token gesture toward nature, because the winery has been very active in conservation. It follows World Wildlife Federation guidelines for sustainable land use, uses no insecticides in the vineyards, and applies only an island-grown natural fertilizer, sorghum sudan grass. It uses renewable energy sources (wind and solar), treats used water, and composts. The winery has undertaken many projects that include re-intro-ducing the southern flying squirrel and conserving a red cedar savannah forest.

The grapes that grow in this environment con-tribute to a remarkable range of wines that are made by Walter Schmoranz and two other winemakers: Martin Janz, who came from Germany in 1996, and Jeff Kah, an Ottawa native and graduate of Niagara College's wine program. The wines include well-made Chardonnay, Riesling, and Pinot Gris, all with good fruit qualities and food-friendly balance, and a crisp Blanc de Blancs made from Seyval Blanc and Vidal. The grapes for this are picked a little underripe and the wine is reminiscent of vinho verde. A rosé, which Schmoranz describes as "very serious," is made from Chambourcin.

OLD WOOD, NEW GROWTH

PAGES 160–61: **A WORKING BARREL ROOM**

As for the reds, there's an attractive Baco Noir with what Schmoranz calls "a bit of wildness," but they really come into their own with the Bordeaux varieties. Even from the cooler vintages, the Cabernet Franc and Cabernet-Merlot blend show quite intense fruit and good complexity. From warmer vintages they're big-bodied, full of dense fruit and other flavours, and have ripe tannins to sustain them for many more years.

Mastronardi Estate Winery

In 2002, Tony and Rino Mastronardi bought a 100-acre (40-hectare) vineyard from Colio Estate Wines, with the intention of ripping out the vines and building greenhouses to expand their vegetable production. Colio wanted to purchase more vineyard land closer to the lake, where the vines would be less affected by frost than in this inland location.

But instead of planting peppers and tomatoes, the Mastronardis planted wind machines and kept the vines. They sell most of the grapes (mostly Bordeaux reds, along with white varieties like Chardonnay, Riesling, Pinot Gris, and Gewürztraminer) to wineries. Part of the harvest is vinified by winemaker Lyse LeBlanc, however, and the Mastronardis plan to open their winery in 2006.

Aleksander Estate

Aleksander Estate is a small, new winery owned by Aleksander Bemben. Born in Poland, he came to Canada with his family in 1982 and has worked at Pelee Island Winery since he arrived. He began planting vines in 2000 and now has five acres (two hectares) in Riesling, Cabernet Franc, Cabernet Sauvignon, and Chambourcin. He supplements his own grapes with Chardonnay and Baco Noir from other regional growers and produced 1,000 cases of wine in 2004.

The vines are located about a kilometre from the lake and have a little altitude, which offers some protection from cold. In 2004–05, the Cabernet Sauvignon suffered some damage, but more than 80 percent came through unscathed. Aleksander Bemben is assisted in the winemaking and other aspects of the winery by his daughter, Izabela, who graduated in biomedical sciences, then the viticulture and oenology course at Brock University.

The Aleksander Estate lineup includes a crisp, clean Riesling and a well-balanced Barrique Chardonnay with rich fruit flavour. An unusual wine is the 100 percent Chambourcin, from the winery's own vineyard. Izabela Bemben says, "It's a surprising wine, fruit-forward and not too tannic." Their Baco Noir is also very well made—gamey, fruity, and smooth-textured. In addition to these, Aleksander Estate makes wines from peaches and raspberries in good, drinkable styles, with full fruit flavour but enough acidity to keep the sweetness in check.

THE WINERIES

Aleksander Estate
1542 County Road 34
Ruthven, ON N0P 2G0
Tel: 519-326-2024

Colchester Ridge Estate Winery
108 County Road 50
Harrow, ON N0R 1G0
Telphone: 519-738-9800

Colio Estate Wines
1 Colio Drive
Harrow, ON N0R 1G0
Tel: 519-738-2241
www.coliowines.com

D'Angelo Estate Winery
5141 Concession 5
Amherstburg, ON N9V 2Y8
Tel: 519-736-7959
www.dangelowinery.com

Erie Shore Vineyard
410 County Road 50 West
Harrow, ON N0R 1G0
Tel: 519-738-9858
www.erieshore.ca

Mastronardi Estate Winery
1193 Concession Road 3 East
Kingsville, ON N9Y 2E5
Tel: 519-796-0491

Muscedere Vineyards
7457 County Road 18
Harrow, ON N0R 1G0
Tel: 519-796-9007

Pelee Island Winery
455 Seacliff Drive
Kingsville, ON N9K 2K5
Tel: 519-733-6551
www.peleeisland.com

Sanson Estate Winery
9238 Walker Road
McGregor, ON N0R 1J0
Tel: 519-726-9609
www.sansonestatewinery.com

Sprucewood Shores Estate Winery
7258 Heritage Road
Harrow, ON N0R 1G0
Tel: 519-738-9253

Viewpointe Estate Winery
151 County Road 50 East
Harrow, ON N0R 1G0
Tel: 519-738-4718
www.viewpointewinery.com

PRINCE EDWARD COUNTY

"WE HAVE SOME OF THE BEST SOIL IN THE WORLD. THE FRENCH HAVE
SCREWED UP THEIR SOIL BECAUSE THEY WOULDN'T PUT ANYTHING BACK
INTO IT."

—JAMES LAHTI
LONG DOG VINEYARD AND WINERY

Prince Edward County is Ontario's newest wine region, but it isn't yet an official Designated Viticultural Area like Niagara Peninsula, Lake Erie North Shore, and Pelee Island. To achieve that status, a region should harvest an average 275 tons (250 tonnes) of grapes a year. Prince Edward County began to approach that in 2002, but a series of tough winters reduced the following harvests dramatically, to under 110 tons (100 tonnes) in 1993 and 1994.

For many skeptical outsiders looking in, that about says it all, as far as Prince Edward County is concerned. From their perspective, growing grapes in the County (as it's known locally) is a kind of extreme sport, and they don't know whether to watch in fascination or look away in horror as another harsh winter kills vines and damages those that survive. They say, in short, that Prince Edward County is just too cold in winter to sustain a viable grape and wine industry.

On the other side are the true believers, like the winemakers and others who have invested money, time, and skill in the County's many vineyards and wineries. They foresee a future when the region produces some of Ontario's great Pinot Noirs and Chardonnays, not to mention other varieties. They're convinced that the County has a unique combination of climate and soils, and that

OPPOSITE: **HOPING FOR A GOOD VINTAGE**

appropriate grape-growing techniques will meet the challenges the climate presents.

Each side can make arguments to support its position. On the negative side is the fact that Prince Edward County has failed to produce sizeable harvests and that harvest size has declined rather than increased. Most of the wine produced in the County is made from grapes grown in the Niagara Peninsula. Some carry the VQA Ontario designation, but that would be true of wine made in Wawa or Ottawa from Niagara grapes. In short, the County's detractors say, producing wine made from grapes grown elsewhere does not a wine region make.

However, it can be argued that if Prince Edward County suffered vine damage and reduced crops in the 2003 and 2005 harvests, so did Niagara Peninsula, where production was down to half the normal volume. Besides, people scoffed for decades at the idea that Niagara could make quality wine, and laughed at the pioneers who planted vinifera there in the 1960s and 1970s. Prince Edward County, the argument goes, simply needs time to match the right varieties to its particular soils and climate and to develop the techniques to protect them in winter.

In fact, many Niagara winery owners and winemakers have supported the endeavours of Prince Edward County's new pioneers. Jean-Pierre Colas of Peninsula Ridge likes the minerality that shows through in many of the white wines, and winemaker Deborah Paskus was the driving force behind the County's Closson Chase winery. Others have offered practical and moral support. County winemaker Norman Hardie, who has broad international experience, says, "Every new region needs a neighbour as a springboard to get it started. Marlborough in New Zealand was springboarded by Hawkes Bay, and then a few years later, Central Otago used Marlborough as a springboard. Niagara is ours."

Between the negative and positive attitudes toward Prince Edward County wine, the middle position of healthy, wait-and-see skepticism is sparsely populated. Time will tell which of the two polar-opposite visions of the County's wine future is right: one of abandoned vineyards, derelict wineries, and winery signs swinging in a near-Arctic wind, or that of healthy vines growing in the warmth of a bucolic County summer and rendering their harvest to winemakers who turn them into elegant wines.

In the meantime, many people are investing time, effort, and money in Prince Edward County's wine potential in the expectation that it will be a viable, and eventually official, viticultural region. They expect not simply that the County will produce very good wines from local grapes—it has already accomplished that—but that Prince Edward County will become Ontario's fourth Designated Viticultural Area, with a sustainable wine industry.

In the meantime, the Prince Edward County Wine-growers Association produces yellow stickers reading "100% Prince Edward County Grown," which grace bottles of wine made exclusively from grapes grown in the County. They have begun to audit County vineyards to ensure that the stickers are applied only to wine that they can certify as made only from County-grown vines. Along with the official VQA Ontario classification, the yellow stickers give consumers more confidence in the quality and provenance of the wine they buy.

Prince Edward County has a history in many respects similar to Niagara's. Many of its settlers in the late 18th and early 19th centuries had lived in colonies that became part of the United States. The United Empire Loyalist heritage shows in the architecture and names of the County, and this history adds to the County's allure as a tourist destination. Like Niagara, the County became a major producer of Ontario's food in the 1800s. At the turn of the 20th century, about a third of the province's canned fruit (especially apples, cherries, and peaches) and vegetables came from here. At their height, there were more than 40 canneries in the County, but the last one closed in the 1990s. In Niagara, two canneries remain of the scores that used to be in operation. Prince Edward County called itself the Garden County, just as St. Catharines, Niagara's main city, calls itself the Garden City.

The County is still an important producer of apples, but the vegetables and other fruit are pretty much gone. An organic market garden, Vickie's Veggies, grows heritage vegetables, including 34 varieties of tomatoes, 12 of sweet peppers, 12 of hot peppers, and seven or eight of eggplant. They're a rich reminder of the variety that used to flourish here.

As for grapes, the recent spurt of plantings began in earnest in the late 1990s. By the year 2000 the area planted in vinifera varieties was less than 20 acres (eight hectares), but by 2005 it had increased 30-fold to more than 600 acres (240 hectares). If the current trend continues, Prince Edward County is expected to have more than 2,000 acres (800 hectares) by 2015. In 2000, there was only one commercial winery in the County. Now there are a dozen, with more poised to open. There are about 40 plantings in the County, too, but not all will become commercial wineries. Some are hobby vineyards, and others sell grapes to wineries.

In 2001 the County's Economic Development Office published a guide to viticulture for aspiring growers and investors. Written by Geoff Heinricks, a Toronto journalist who moved to the County to become "a 21st-century peasant," it was realistic about the severity of the winters, but optimistic about the prospects for good Pinot Noir from the area. The focus on Pinot Noir and Chardonnay, the principal grapes of Burgundy, is inspired mainly by the County's soil structure. Like Burgundy, Prince Edward County lies on a limestone base, and in some areas limestone rocks stud the upper layers of the soil. In the western half of the County, around Hillier, there are deposits of heavy clay loam, which drain well and are well-suited to vines. The fact that Burgundy and Prince Edward County lie on the same latitude has buttressed the belief that Pinot Noir and Chardonnay should grow well here.

The main difference between Burgundy and the County, of course, is climate. County summers are warm and the growing season is good, as witness the fruit. Prince Edward County has long been an attraction for summer tourism, and tens of thousands of people visit Sandbanks Provincial Park, which has the largest freshwater sand dunes in the world. But the winter temperatures are problematic for viticulture. Mike Peddlesden, who planted vines in the Hillier district in 1999 and now manages the vineyards at The Grange Estate Winery, says,

"Heat and growing season, the County's got. It's the damned winters!" There are significant variations from site to site in the County, but in most areas temperatures drop well below –13°F (–25°C) for at least a few hours each winter—more than cold enough to damage vinifera vines, if not kill them. The lake offers moderating influences during the

VINES NETTED AGAINST BIRDS

year, but in winter most of the shallow waters around the County freeze and don't provide the effect that, most years, protects the vineyards of the Niagara Peninsula from extreme cold.

To deal with the winter, all County growers bury their vinifera vines, and some bury the hybrids, too. Others have also installed wind machines to keep frigid air from settling. Several growers are experimenting with different clones of Chardonnay and Pinot Noir, to see which survive the cold best. Others have planted cold-hardy hybrid varieties, and a couple of producers have already made very promising wines with Vidal and other hybrids. But there's a general recognition that if Prince Edward County is to prosper as a wine region, its main wines must be made from the more highly valued vinifera varieties.

Despite the challenges, the owners of vineyards and wineries of Prince Edward County have several advantages. One of the most important is that the County isn't an established wine region trying to renew itself. Earlier experiments with grapes and wine in the 1800s are of historical interest only, and today's County grape growers and winemakers have the opportunity to invent a wine region from scratch. Perhaps this explains the influx of prospective winemakers and winery investors, most from Toronto, which is only 120 miles (200 kilometres) away. Many observers have expressed amazement at the number of people investing so much time, effort, and money in an untried region. It's possible that the sense of adventure and challenge of being a pioneer in what might become a success story outweighs the caution normally expected of people with money to invest. And those who might have invested in wine in Niagara find vineyard land a lot less expensive in the County. They're part of a broader movement of immigrants, most from the Toronto area, who have bought land and built cottages and retirement homes. Their massive houses, with boat ramps and multi-car garages, dot the shoreline of the County.

Time will show how wise many of them were to clear land, plant vines, and construct wineries. But while the passage of time marks progress, time itself achieves nothing. The emergence of a viable, successful wine region in Prince Edward County rests on the climate and on the passion and work of the women and men who are putting their mark on the land and their imprint on the County's wines.

INTO THE CRUSHER

THE WINERIES OF
PRINCE EDWARD COUNTY

By Chadsey's Cairns Winery and Vineyard

Prince Edward County's wineries are widely dispersed, but half of them are in the Hillier District at the western end of the peninsula. One of those looks like a conventional farm, with a heritage farmhouse and barns and a small flock of Cotswold sheep in the field bordering the road. By Chadsey's Cairns Winery and Vineyard is so-named because the vineyard is planted near a series of stone cairns erected in the 1800s by Ira Chadsey. Chadsey believed that he'd be reincarnated after his death as a white horse. The cairns were a navigational aid, to guide him back to his farm. So far, there's been no sighting of Chadsey, who committed suicide in 1905. But if he does return, he'll find that the farm's present owners, Richard Johnston and Vida Zalnieriunas, have complicated his landing by planting 19 acres (eight hectares) of Riesling, Gamay, Chardonnay, Gewürztraminer, Pinot Noir, Chenin Blanc, Muscat, and St. Laurent.

Neither Johnston nor Zalnieriunas seems a likely candidate as grape grower or winemaker. He was an educator and a member of the Ontario legislature for several years, and she's a psychotherapist, but they bought a two centuries-old, 215-acre (85-hectare) farm. Vida describes the genesis of the vineyard this way: "The reality is I'm married to a romantic workaholic. The first time Richard walked into the field . . . he said, 'I think you can grow grapes here.' He said it in a kind of wistful, let's-do-it way. I said, 'Are you crazy? Do you know how much work that is?' We had this conversation for three years, until I finally relented. Speaking professionally, all that stuff about living off the farm is a Freudian post-rationalization defence mechanism at work. He wanted to walk in vineyards."

Johnston and Zalnieriunas planted their first vines, Riesling, in 1998, placing them among the first to start cultivating vinifera in the County. Their first vintage was 2002, and they opened the winery in 2003. The farm also has a small, one-room brick building originally used by Ira Chadsey to store apples, which was later a schoolhouse and

NEW GROWTH

church. It's now the winery tasting room and shop, and there's a pleasant view of the vineyard from a deck that has been added to the back. The farm also has a small, fenced pioneer cemetery, with the oldest legible headstone dating to 1805.

By Chadsey's Cairns is located close enough to Lake Ontario that it gets some moderating effects, but in winter the temperature can still drop to –17°F (–27°C). "It's extreme viticulture," Zalnieriunas says, and they bury the vines each year. With assistance from consultant winemaker, Martin Gemmrich, and now from Ann Sperling, she has become what she describes as "an accidental winemaker."

Johnston and Zalnieriunas buy some grapes from Niagara, but most of their wine is made from their own vineyard in a winery located in one of the barns. Their vines have produced a quite astringent Gamay with solid fruit flavours and earthy notes, and an impressive Pinot Noir with dark fruit flavours and very firm tannins. A Cabernet Franc from young vines showed surprisingly intense fruit flavours and rich tannins, with good acidity.

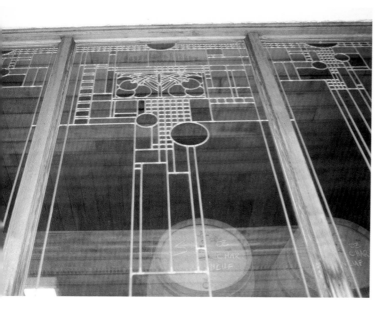

WINE FERMENTING IN BARRELS BEHIND WINE-THEMED STAINED GLASS

Sandbanks Estate Winery

Close to By Chadsey's Cairns is Sandbanks Estate Winery, whose owner, Catherine Langlois, has a lineage that goes as deep as any in Canada's wine history. In 1535, the French explorer Samuel de Champlain discovered wild grapes growing on an island in the St. Lawrence River. He named the island Île de Bacchus, after the Roman god of wine, although he later changed it to Île d'Orléans, in honour of his patron, the Duke of Orléans.

Catherine Langlois was born on the Île d'Orléans, and her journey upstream, from Champlain's island of grapes to her vineyard in Prince Edward County, took her first to Montreal and then to Burgundy. She started a career in hotel management in Montreal, but in 1994 won a bursary to study and work in the wine industry in Burgundy. When she returned to Canada she imagined getting a job in a winery cellar in Niagara. However, she was offered a sales position in Ottawa for a large Ontario winery, and she took it, partly because Ottawa is bilingual.

As Langlois learned more about Ontario wines and heard about the vines being planted in Prince Edward County, less than three hours' drive from Ottawa, she began to look for a suitable location for a vineyard. In 1999, she bought land near the shore just west of Wellington, and she and her family moved to the County the next year. They built a house and planted six acres (2.5 hectares) of vines: mostly Vidal, Baco Noir, Riesling, and Cabernet Franc, as well as some Geisenheim, Pinot Noir, and Maréchal Foch.

The Sandbanks vines are planted on a south-facing incline within sight of Lake Ontario, which moderates the temperature during the year. They're rooted in soil made up of well-drained clay and limestone rock. Catherine Langlois says she has worked hard with her land, and is very happy with it so far. She buries her vinifera vines only, and says the key is getting them out in spring as early as possible. Being so close to the lake, her vines are at minimal risk of late frosts.

She made her first vintage in 2003, using only her own grapes. In principle, she wants to make wine exclusively from her own fruit, although she did buy a little Chardonnay in 2004. That year, Sandbanks produced nearly 400 cases, and in 2005, nearly 500. As for how much she plans to make, Langlois says it depends on the weather and the yield each year. Since she started, the climate has been erratic, and she says very reasonably, "We're not sure what a real crop looks like in Prince Edward County."

Langlois sold her first vintages only to restaurants, especially in Ottawa, but in 2006 she obtained a retail licence. It isn't that she has had any trouble selling her wine: it has readily sold out. In fact, she says, "We were looking at the Cabernet Franc the other day, and I said, 'I don't want to sell any more. I want to be able to drink some of it all winter long.'"

Carmela Estates Winery

A few minutes' drive slightly inland from Sandbanks Winery is Norman Hardie country. Norman Hardie is Prince Edward County's most experienced resident winemaker, having made wine in South Africa, Burgundy, New Zealand, California, and Oregon. In Prince Edward County, he's involved in two wineries, Carmela Estates and his own, nearby, called simply Norman Hardie.

Carmela Estates in Hillier started life as Peddlesden Estate, named for Michael Peddlesden, who headed a group of investors in the vineyard. They planted 30 acres (12 hectares) in 1999 and opened the winery in 2002 with a retail store, restaurant, and winemaking facilities, partly underground, where natural temperatures are 41°F (5°C) in winter and 57°–64°F (14°–16°C) in summer. Peddlesden Estate was later purchased from the founding consortium by Bob and Sherry Tompkins, who renamed it for Sherry's mother.

The vineyard is planted with Pinot Noir, by far the most important variety, as well as Chardonnay, Riesling, Pinot Gris, and Cabernet Franc. The wines reflect these varieties, although some grapes are purchased from Niagara. In general, Carmela Estates' wines have been very well received and many sell out quickly. The Cabernet Franc, which combines Niagara and County fruit, has very typical flavours and a long finish, and the Riesling, also an inter-regional blend, has attractive tropical flavours.

Norman Hardie Winery

Across the road, at his own winery, Norman Hardie planted 15,000 vines on his eight-acre (three-hectare) property in 2002 and 2003. Eighty percent are Pinot Noir, with the rest divided equally between

169

Chardonnay and Pinot Gris—the varieties Hardie believes match his soil best. His vineyard is planted on such well-drained clay that he could say, in August 2005, "we had three-quarters of an inch of rain here last night, and we could walk in the vineyards this morning. It tells us how fabulously drained the vineyard is."

The Norman Hardie winery was completed and opened in 2005. It has winemaking facilities, a tasting area, and space for a restaurant. It's built on a ridge, which not only allows for good views but enables the winemaking process to be gravity fed. The grapes are crushed outside, then flow to tanks on the lower level where the winemaking area has several interesting features. Rather than the vertical fermenting tanks that you usually see in wineries, Hardie's are horizontal. They were originally used in a dairy for storing milk, but now they hold Chardonnay and Pinot Gris (much more interesting beverages). Hardie likes his white wines to rest on their lees (dead yeast cells and other solids) for extended periods, and the horizontal tanks offer a much better wine-to-lees ratio than vertical tanks, giving his wines that much more complexity.

The highlight is the barrel room, which is partly underground. It has been constructed to expose part of the limestone ridge, which protrudes into the cellar along the base of one wall. There it bleeds water and provides the cellar with natural humidity. "It's a fabulous feature," Hardie acknowledges, "but it was an engineering nightmare." It provides year-round humidity of 75–82 percent, which is ideal. "You lose less wine to the angels," Hardy says, a reference to the wine that evaporates through the pores of the barrels more quickly when the humidity is low.

The cool, damp conditions delay malolactic fermentation (which softens wine's acidity) until the spring. Hardie is a big believer that malolactic fermentation is best delayed, not started right after the first fermentation, which converts sugars to alcohol. "The primary fermentation is vigorous, and it's best to allow the wine to recuperate and rest, and then go through malolactic when nature warms up in spring. It's more in harmony with nature."

At present, Hardie sources about 70 percent of his grapes from Niagara, and 30 percent from his own and other Prince Edward County vineyards. As his vines mature, they'll contribute more, but he foresees settling at about half Niagara and half County fruit. He's a realist, he says, and "it's not business savvy to put all your eggs in one basket." As he sees it, it's not a problem for him to vinify Niagara grapes in the County or to blend wines from the two regions. In California, he points out, "Napa wineries bring grapes from Sonoma . . . If we make good wine here, it all helps the whole Ontario wine industry."

Hardie buries his vines during the winter and has had excellent survival rates: he estimates 96–97 percent of his vines survived the 2004–05 winter. He aims to produce 3,000 to 5,000 cases of wine a year by 2010, but says it all depends on the quality of the grapes. "If we don't have a great year, I'll back off. If we have a great growing season, I'll go ahead. It's all quality driven." Hardie's first wines from his own vines were released in late 2005 and the spring of 2006. In the meantime he produced impressive Pinot Noirs and Chardonnays from Niagara fruit, and lovely Riesling and Vidal from County-grown vines.

The Grange of Prince Edward County Estate Winery

North of Norman Hardie's winery, in the rolling countryside near the eastern end of Consecon Lake, are two more wineries. The first of these, The Grange of Prince Edward County Estate Winery, draws its name from two sources: it's located in a grange (a farm building for storing grain) and it was founded by two Grangers, Robert and his daughter, Caroline. Robert Granger was a Toronto lawyer before he retired to Prince Edward County, where he bought the original loyalist homestead of the Trumpour family in 1974. Caroline persuaded him to plant vines on this farm near Hillier and, starting in 2001, they've planted 50 acres (20 hectares).

The stress is on the Burgundy varieties, again largely because of the soil, which is clay gravel on fractured limestone. Pinot Noir rules—it accounts for about half the vines—but there's a good representation of Chardonnay, as well as Gamay, Pinot Gris, Cabernet Franc, and Riesling. The winery facilities are located in a massive, finely-restored grange that dates back to 1826. The tasting room is in the former loft, where a floor-to-ceiling fireplace made from fieldstones has been added. The former milking room is now the barrel room, and the stable has become the bottling room.

The Grange has employed a winemaker to work year-round since the first vintage. Jeff Innes started in Niagara in 1996 and made wine at Reif Estate, Vineland Estate, and Harbour Estate, before leaving in 2001. He did a harvest in Georgia in 2002, and came to The Grange in 2003, when the winery was being constructed. The seriousness of The Grange's stress on Burgundy is shown by the fact that they have a consultant winemaker from Burgundy to work with Innes on the Pinot Noir and Chardonnay.

Niagara grapes are supplementing The Grange's own until their vines mature. Under their Trumpour's Mill label, they produced 1,500 cases of wine in 2003, 3,600 in 2004, and are aiming at 25,000 cases sometime in the future. This will mean expanding their vineyards from the present size.

Trumpour's Mill wines made from Prince Edward County fruit include a summery rosé made from their own Pinot Noir and Gamay, and a Gamay made in the Beaujolais method. There are also two Trumpour's Mill blends, a red (Baco Noir, Chambourcin, and Castell) and a white (Riesling, Pinot Gris, Chardonnay, and Melon de Bourgogne) that is crisp with aromatic lemon-lime flavours. Jeff Innes says it started as a house white, "but maybe it's better than that."

Closson Chase Vineyards

The neighbouring winery is Closson Chase, named for its location on the intersection of Closson and

WINTER PRUNING

FILLING THE BINS

Chase Roads. The winemaking facilities and tasting bar are located in a 100-year-old barn, and the barrel room is in a former pig barn. The winery, which opened for business in mid-2005, has celebrity associations. For the wine-savvy, the draw is Closson Chase winemaker Deborah Paskus, one of Niagara's best-known (and current winemaker at Tawse Winery). For the media-savvy, it's television star Sonja Smits ("Street Legal," "Traders") and former partner in Alliance Atlantis Communications Seaton McLean, both co-owners of Closson Chase.

Closson Chase has two vineyards, and they planted the first in Chardonnay and Pinot Noir. They plan to have 30 acres (12 hectares) in vines by 2010. The owners are convinced that these varieties will do well in their location "because they like the soil," but they're resigned to having to baby-sit the vines. Even when they bury the canes they have been losing 50 percent of the buds, and during the growing season the grapes are at risk from deer, birds, raccoons, and hornets.

Their first experiences with vines weren't promising. In 2002, the grapes were eaten by birds, and the following year even the birds lost out because the raccoons got there first. That year, too, a shipment of vines from France was lost at sea. On the positive side (once the vines are in and protected from local wildlife) are the County soil and a dry, warm mid-season. Still, Seaton McLean talks about the innovative drive that underlies the start not only of Closson Chase, but of other County wineries. "With that pioneering spirit comes both the fear of the unknown and the joy of discovery."

Closson Chase aims to produce up to 6,000 cases of wine a year once it's in full swing and plans to add a Pinot Noir-based sparkling wine to its line. Until its own vines are mature, the winery is making wine from grapes grown on the Beamsville Bench in Niagara. The first three vintages of Closson Chase Chardonnay (2001 to 2003) wore their Niagara vintages well. All the Chardonnays are barrel-fermented and aged for 18 months in new and used French barrels, while the Pinot Noir gets 12 to 18 months.

Huff Estates

Drive from Closson Chase toward Picton and on your left you'll see what is by far the most impressive-looking winery in Prince Edward County: Huff Estates, which opened in 2004. Seen from the road, it wouldn't be out of place in Napa Valley—a low-lying, stylish, concrete structure with good use of glass. The tasting room is all light and opens out on a patio with a small waterfall. A 20-room boutique hotel, The Inn at Huff Estates, will cater to visitors, and those on a tight schedule can come and go by helicopter, using Huff's helipad.

The passion and money behind all this effort is Lanny Huff. His family traces its roots in Prince Edward County back to the 1820s, when the Huffs arrived as United Empire Loyalists. The intersection near the winery at Highway 62 and County Road 1 is informally known as Huff's Corner. Lanny Huff was successful in the plastics industry, and his winery combines his commitment to Prince Edward County and his love of wine.

Huff Estates has 40 acres (16 hectares) planted on three sites. One vineyard, with Chardonnay, Vidal, and Castell, surrounds the winery, and another nearby is planted only with Chardonnay. The third is 18 miles (30 kilometers) away at South Bay. Its waterside location gives more warmth, and the varieties planted there include Chardonnay, Pinot Gris, Merlot, Cabernet Franc, and Cabernet Sauvignon. The soil there is distinct, too—clay on limestone—and Huff likens it to Pomerol in Bordeaux, which is famed for its Merlot. For that reason, Huff planted Merlot vines in the South Bay vineyard, the only Merlot in the County. He also buys grapes from five other growers in the County and from Niagara Peninsula.

As for the winery, it has state-of-the-art equipment and a well-stocked, gravity-fed barrel room with capacity for 250 barriques. Right now the winemaker, Frédéric Picard, is experimenting with a variety of barrels. The winery produced 2,000

NEW GROWTH VINE

cases of wine in 2003, 4,000 in 2004, and is aiming for 8,000 to 10,000 by 2010. They've been buying some grapes from Niagara until their own vines come on stream, but they expect to make Huff Estate wine exclusively from Prince Edward County fruit from the 2008 vintage.

Huff Estate's Chardonnays, aged in a variety of barrels, are promising and the Pinot Gris, from young vines in the South Bay vineyard, has typical aromatics with nice body and texture. Among the reds, there are lighter-styled Bordeaux blends combining Cabernet Sauvignon, Cabernet Franc, and Merlot. Frédéric Picard is optimistic about the wines he'll make from Huff's vineyards. "The key word in winemaking," he says, "is patience." He's working on some experimental batches of wine and plans to add a late-harvest Vidal to the Huff lineup.

Black Prince Winery

Closer to Picton, on the Loyalist Parkway, is Black Prince Winery. When the founders were casting about for a winery name, they thought of Prince Edward County Winery but dismissed it as too bland and generic. Some research turned up Prince Edward, eldest son of King Edward III of England, who ruled over part of Aquitaine, including Bordeaux, in the 14th century.

The combination of Prince Edward and Bordeaux was irresistible, and because Edward was known as the "Black Prince" (probably because he wore a suit of black armour in battle), the winery got its name. A suit of armour stands (empty) in the winery retail shop and, in keeping with the theme, Black Prince Winery holds an annual medieval jousting tournament at the culmination of Ontario Wine Week, in the third week of June.

VINES AFTER RAIN

This winery was founded in 2000 when John Sambrook, who then ran the Opimian Society, decided to invest in this up-and-coming wine region. The Opimian Society is a wine club that offers wines exclusively to its 15,000 or so members across Canada. The Society's membership is a potential market for Black Prince wines that other County wineries might envy: even before the first Black Prince bottle rolled off the bottling-line, orders for more than 2,000 cases were in hand. Looking at the quality of other wines in Prince Edward County, the Opimian Society has included wines from Huff Estates and Sandbanks Estate in its offers.

The nine-acre (3.5-hectare) vineyard that lies behind the winery is planted with Chardonnay, Riesling, Auxerrois, Chambourcin, Pinot Noir, Cabernet Franc, and Maréchal Foch. Black Prince also buys from other growers in the County, as well as from Niagara, and has purchased Vidal grapes from Lake Erie North Shore for its icewine. The

winery's Californian winemaker, Michael Fallow, visits regularly. In 2004 and 2005, Black Prince made a little under 5,000 cases of wine, of which 1,000 were exclusively County grapes and 1,600 were a blend of grapes from the County and other Ontario regions. It's aiming for production of about 10,000 cases a year.

The first Black Prince vintage, 2002, bore a First Crush label. The wines included a Baco Noir, which brought together Prince Edward County Baco Noir and Cabernet Franc, including some of the winery's own fruit, and a 2002 Vidal, a blend of County Vidal and components of all the white varieties in the Black Prince vineyard. There was also an estate-grown Auxerrois, a variety that Black Prince general manager Geoffrey Webb says "could become the banner white grape" of Prince Edward County. Both the 2003 and 2004 vintages sold out before the end of August.

Black Prince's 2004 vintage was touch and go until the end. The preceding winter was very cold and the summer cool and wet. But then, Webb notes, there occurred "the kind of miracle that many think only happens in Bordeaux. The skies cleared, the temperatures soared, and for six glorious weeks, the grapes sped to maturity and suddenly harvesting began one to two weeks earlier than in 2003."

Long Dog Vineyard & Winery

Southeast of Picton, near the hamlet of Milford, James Lahti and his partners make wine at Long Dog Vineyards & Winery. If Prince Edward County is going to make its name with Pinot Noir, Lahti, an IMAX filmmaker and a passionate devotee of Pinot Noir, is one of those who'll share the glory. He cultivates 20 acres (eight hectares) of vines on a 300-acre (120-hectare) farm that he, his wife, Victoria Rose, and a friend, Steven Rapkin, bought in 1997 as a weekend getaway when they lived in Toronto. Lahti and his wife spent more and more time there; he built a film-editing studio in a barn and began to think about planting grapes.

As Victoria Rose tells it, "In 1999, an enthusiastic James and a slightly skeptical Steven and I planted 1,200 vines—Chardonnay, Pinot Noir, Pinot Blanc,

and Gamay. As we watched them thrive in the hot, dry summer and delicious limestone dirt, James decided to plant another 3,700 vines in the spring of 2000 . . ." They opened the winery in 2004 and named it after the Lahtis' wire-haired dachshunds.

What persuaded Lahti to plant vines was the terroir, which reminded him of Burgundy's. The County was on the right latitude, it had the right combination of warm days and cool nights during the growing season, and the underlying rock was limestone. "We have some of the best soil in the world," he says. In fact, he goes on, the soil is better than the French, which is too acidic. "The French have screwed up their soil because they wouldn't put anything back into it."

About half of Lahti's vines are Pinot Noir, a third are Chardonnay, and the rest are Pinot Gris, with a little Pinot Blanc. Lahti made about 1,000 cases of his first vintage, in 2002. That was an excellent year and produced "amazing heat units," with the temperature rising above 85°F (30°C) on more than 50 days. That year's barrel-fermented Chardonnay had rich tropical flavours with mineral notes, and some of the Pinot Noirs offered quite elegant fruit and structure. Lahti experimented with a variety of French and Hungarian barrels.

The following winters were more difficult, but many Long Dog wines are showing well. A VQA Ontario Chardonnay from Lahti's oldest vines had quite intense flavours, and his Pinot Grigio was impressive. The standard-bearing Pinot Noirs from the Long Dog vineyard have good fruit, and Lahti gets nice variations on a Burgundian theme from his ensemble of barrels from different coopers. Lahti is planting more vines and plans to increase production to 4,000 cases. If current sales are anything to go by, he'll sell all his production, because there are waiting lists of people wanting to buy his wine.

Waupoos Estates Winery

Two more commercial wineries are located nearby at Waupoos, at the eastern end of the County. Ed Neuser, co-owner of Waupoos Estates, was the first person to take the leap into commercial viticulture in Prince Edward County. He planted a vineyard in

1993 and says people in the area muttered about "that crazy German." At first it seemed they might have been right: that winter, the temperature fell to –33°F (–36°C), hardly auspicious for grapes. But Neuser is stubborn; he persevered with the vines and opened the winery in 2001. Today he makes white and red wines from his own 20 acres (eight

THE CRUSH

hectares) of grapes, as well as bringing Cabernet, Gamay, and Merlot grapes from Niagara.

A crusty individualist, Neuser came to Canada from Germany in 1957 and worked at odd jobs in Ottawa for a year. From there he made a career in the steel industry, working in factories in Montreal but mainly in the Toronto area. In 1983, he discovered Prince Edward County and put in an offer on a big apple orchard. He was surprised to get it but didn't move to the County from Toronto until 2000, when he went into semi-retirement.

Neuser and his partner, Rita Kaimins, whose career was in merchandising and buying ladies' wear for clothing and department stores, both love good food and wine. They thought it a good idea to plant some vines and make wine for their own pleasure. Neuser ran the idea by his friend Klaus Reif,

of Niagara's Reif Estate, who said, "Why not?" They were joined in the venture by a young man, then only 17 years old, who grew up in the County. Kyle Baldwin is now manager of the estate, and oversees all plantings, pruning, and maintenance, as well as winemaking.

Some of the wines in the quite astonishing range on the shelves of his retail store are made from Niagara grapes, but most are made from Waupoos' own vines. They include both vinifera and hybrids: Vidal, Seyval Blanc, Geisenheim, Riesling, Chardonnay, Pinot Gris, and Gewürztraminer in the whites, and De Chaunac, Baco Noir, St. Laurent, and Pinot Noir in the reds. The winery also makes "Waupoos Winter Wine" in the traditional icewine style.

Neuser had the foresight to think of wine as a tourist pursuit. He not only opened a winery but installed an impressive retail store and tasting counter from which he sells 4,000 cases of wine a year. From the store, visitors can walk between vineyards to the Gazebo Restaurant, which offers vine and lake views. Each month during the summer, about 10,000 people come to the winery, most by car and bus, but many by boat, because Waupoos also has its own docking facilities.

County Cider Company

If Ed Neuser planted his grapes first, his neighbour just along the road, Grant Howes, opened the first winery in Prince Edward County, in 1997. For Howes it represented a return to a farming life. He grew up in the County, left the area to work as a business consultant, then returned in the 1990s and opened the County Cider Company in 1996, in order to develop his family's 150-year-old apple orchard. Soon after, he took land near his cidery and planted Pinot Noir, Chardonnay, Gamay, and Zweigelt, as well as some white German hybrids. He has another vineyard in Adolfustown planted in a range of vines that includes Cabernet Franc. While his vines were growing, Howes sourced grapes from Niagara and began selling wine in 1997. He bought Niagara grapes until 2002 and then decided to make wine only from his own vines.

The County Cider Company, located on a lime-stone ridge overlooking the lake, has one of the best views in the County. The tasting room (and restaurant in summer) is in a stone barn that dates to 1832. You can have lunch on the patio with a glass of Howes' wine, and enjoy the vista of vines and water.

Howes' un-oaked Chardonnay, made from grapes grown in the Adolfustown vineyard near the lake-shore, has delicate flavours with mineral notes. His Prinyers Cuvée, a blend of Pinot Noir and Gamay, is a light-bodied red with quite flavourful cherry and plum fruit. He also has an interesting blend of Castell, Baco Noir, and Chambourcin that offers flavours of sweet dark fruit, tobacco, and beets. The Castell contributes quite distinct flavours to the blend, Howes says. The raccoons certainly appreciate them, because they ate all the Castell grapes in 2002.

Howes' annual production of 500 to 600 cases of wine is only about a 20th of his cider output. He also produces a stunning dessert cider that's made in much the same way as icewine. The apples are left on the tree to freeze, then are crushed frozen so as to release concentrated, sweet juice. That juice is then frozen, which solidifies much of the water in it, and the residual viscous juice is poured off and fermented for several months to about 10 percent alcohol. In flavour intensity, the iced cider compares well with icewine.

Sugarbush Vineyards

Many more County winemakers making wine from their own fruit are poised to go commercial. They include Robert and Sally Peck of Sugarbush Vineyards, who planted eight and a half acres (3.4 hectares) in the Hillier district between The Grange and Huff Estates, in 2002. Their vines are all vinifera: Riesling, Chardonnay, Gewürztraminer, Pinot Noir, Gamay, and Cabernet Franc. They planned to pick a first, small crop in 2004, but the raccoons beat them to it. They've installed electric fences to deal with the raccoons and hope to have some wine ready to serve in a tasting room in 2006.

The Pecks got the wine bug when they visited the Okanagan Valley a few years ago. Sally Peck

says, "We thought it was a really nice lifestyle and said to ourselves, 'Can you imagine owning a win-ery?'" They lived in Calgary at that time, but Robert Peck grew up in Prince Edward County, and on a visit there they heard about the vineyards being planted. They decided to buy land while it was

BARREL-FERMENTING

PAGE 179: **GRAPES IN GLASS**

PAGES 180–81: **THE FLAT PLAIN OF NIAGARA-ON-THE-LAKE**

affordable and plan to extend their vineyard over the next few years.

There are many other vineyards in Prince Edward County. Expect to see more labels appearing with names like Red Tail, Black River, Hillier Creek, and Rosehall Run.

THE WINERIES

Black Prince Winery
13370 Loyalist Parkway
Picton, ON K0K 2T0
Tel: 613-476-4888
www.blackprincewinery.com

By Chadsey's Cairns Winery & Vineyard
17432 Loyalist Parkway
Wellington, ON K0K 3L0
Tel: 613-399-2992
www.bychadseyscairns.com

Carmela Estates Winery
1186 Greer Road
Wellington, ON K0K 3L0
Tel: 613-399-3939
www.carmelaestates.ca

Closson Chase Vineyards
629 Closson Road
Hillier, ON K0K 2J0
Tel: 613-399-1418
www.clossonchase.com

County Cider Company
County Road 8
Picton, ON K0K 2T0
Tel: 613-476-1022
www.countycider.com

**The Grange of Prince
Edward Inc. Estate Winery**
990 Closson Road
Hillier, ON K0K 2J0
Tel: 613-399-1048
www.thegrangewines.com

Huff Estates
2274 County Road 1
Bloomfield, ON K0K 1G0
Tel: 613-393-5802
www.huffestates.com

Long Dog Vineyard & Winery
104 Brewers Road
Milford, ON K0K 2P0
Tel: 613-476-4140
www.longdog.ca

Norman Hardie Winery
1172 Greer Road
Wellington, ON K0K 3L0
Tel: 613-827-1204

Sandbanks Estate Winery
17598 Loyalist Parkway
Wellington, ON K0K 3L0
Tel: 613-399-1839

Sugarbush Vineyards
1286 Wilson Road
Hillier, ON K0K 2J0
Tel: 613-849-0521
www.sugarbushvineyards.ca

Waupoos Estates Winery
3016 County Road 8
Picton, ON K0K 2T0
Tel: 613-476-8338
www.waupooswinery.com

TORONTO AND THE REST OF ONTARIO

"A QUALITY BOTTLE OF ONTARIO-GROWN, PRODUCED, AND CELLARED WINE DOESN'T HAVE TO BE EXPENSIVE."

—JAMIE QUAI
QUAI DU VIN ESTATE WINERY

Almost all of Ontario's wineries are located in one of the province's three Designated Viticultural Areas (Niagara Peninsula, Lake Erie North Shore, and Pelee Island) or in Prince Edward County, which aspires to become the fourth. A handful more are located in the Toronto area, close enough to Niagara (a two-hour drive) that they can truck grapes from there for vinification. Other wineries are dotted across the Ontario countryside southwest of Toronto and also to the east as far as Ottawa. These wineries produce wine from grapes and other fruit.

Southbrook Winery

One winery that has successfully combined wine production from grapes and fruit is Southbrook Winery, located between Richmond Hill and Maple, about 15 miles north of Toronto. The owner, Bill Redelmeier, opted for a site on his farm, rather than purchasing land in Niagara, and used existing farm buildings—a pair of century-old barns—to house the tasting room and the barrel room. It was not only a good financial plan but also made good commercial sense to stay on the farm because he can sell his wines at the market store where he sells his other produce. The 285-acre (115–hectare) Southbrook Farm is a major attraction in the area and receives between 100,000 and 125,000 visitors a year.

OPPOSITE: **SPRING GROWTH**

Redelmeier used to have Canada's largest Jersey dairy herd, and he also grows berries and vegetables, but he was as much in love with wine as with cows and pumpkins, and opened his winery in 1991. The first wines were made from berries, and Southbrook Framboise, a raspberry-based dessert wine, has a keen following, even among those short-sighted wine lovers who sneer at fruit wines. Southbrook also makes wines from blueberries, blackberries, and black currants, and from rare golden raspberries grown in Niagara.

On the wine side of the business, Redelmeier buys grapes from Niagara growers, and produces Chardonnay, Sauvignon Blanc, Vidal, the Cabernets, Merlot, and Maréchal Foch under the Southbrook name. Most are bottled as varietals and some are vineyard designated. In addition to the berry-based dessert wines, Southbrook makes an icewine from Vidal. Southbrook produces about 12,000 cases of wine a year and has a reserve level called Triomphe.

The first winemaker was Derek Barnett, who trained in England as a dairy agronomist before trying his hand—with superlative results—at winemaking. In 2000 he became a partner in and winemaker for Lailey Vineyard, which supplies Southbrook with some of its premium grapes. Southbrook's present winemaker is Colin Campbell, who has been there for more than 10 years and took over as winemaker in 2001. Among his wines are two entry-level wines made mainly from Vidal and Maréchal Foch, but the premium wines are all vinifera-based. The consistently successful Triomphe Sauvignon Blanc is aged in oak for a short period, and Southbrook's Lailey Vineyard Chardonnay is reliable year after year. The pure fruit in Southbrook's Pinot Noir always achieves good complexity, and the Watson Vineyard Cabernet Franc, sourced from Niagara-on-the-Lake, has quite intense flavours.

Cilento Wines

Over in Woodbridge, Cilento Wines grew out of a business run by Grace and Angelo Locilento that sold grapes and juice to home winemakers. But Grace says that owning a winery had been in her mind since she was small because she grew up in Italy and her grandmother owned a vineyard. The Locilentos started producing wine in 1993, and opened the California Mission-style winery in Woodbridge in 1997.

The first winemaker was Ann Sperling, who's now executive winemaker at Niagara's Malivoire Wine Company. She was succeeded by Terence van Rooyen, a South African whose notable Cilento wines were Sauvignon Blanc, Riesling, Chardonnay and Merlot. He became winemaker at Niagara's Stonechurch Winery in late 2004.

Cilento sources grapes from the Niagara region for the 25,000 cases it produces each year. The decision to locate the winery north of Toronto and truck grapes to the winery was made because the Locilentos have other business interests in the North Toronto area and because of the "proximity of the Italian community in Woodbridge, which provides a good market for Cilento wines." Cilento did have its own vineyard in Niagara-on-the-Lake, from which it sourced grapes for its Sauvignon Blanc, but sold it to Stonechurch in 2004.

Vinoteca Winery

Another Woodbridge winery is Vinoteca, founded by Giovanni Follegot in 1989. In 1992 Follegot and his wife, Rosanna, bought vineyards near Beamsville on a variety of locations on the Bench and lakeshore. On one of them near the lake they constructed the Maple Grove Vinoteca Estate Winery, where they grow a small range of varieties and some Vidal for icewine. In Woodbridge the emphasis is on entry-level wines sold in large formats, with some blends that include wines from Italian vineyards owned by the Follegots.

Willow Springs Winery

In Stouffville, near Markham, Willow Springs Winery produces 2,500 cases of wine a year from grapes grown on its 11 acres (4.5 hectares) of vineyards. The winery was a lifelong dream of Mario and Julie Testa, who planted the vines on the family's beef cattle farm in 1996. Mario Testa grew up in Ontario as the son of immigrants from Italy and as a child helped his father make wine at home. He's now in

FUNGICIDE SPRAYING IN FALL'S
LAST MONTH OF GROWTH

retail grocery but spends weekends at the winery. The vines are a mix of hybrid and vinifera varieties: Seyval Blanc, Frontenac, Saverois, Maréchal Foch, Baco Noir, Geisenheim, Chardonnay, and Pinot Gris. Testa buys Bordeaux red grapes from a vineyard in Niagara-on-the-Lake, and in 2004 bought Vidal to make icewine for the first time. He makes as much VQA wine as the regulations allow, given his grape varieties.

Willow Springs is located on the Oakridge Moraine in a microclimate that gives a slightly longer growing season in the fall than neighbouring areas. Even so, there's a likelihood of frost in the third or fourth week of September, so the vines are all early-ripening. There was an initial problem with drainage (the area has a high water table) but it was solved by installing field tiles.

One of Willow Springs' marketing advantages is that it's located in the Greater Toronto Area (GTA).

Bus tours regularly stop at the winery, and it's popular for weddings and other functions. Two of the wines, a Cabernet Franc and a Chardonnay, were sold in LCBO Vintages stores, and two others, (Baco Noir and Chardonnay) were selected by the LCBO for sale in 60 stores in the Toronto area. The wines are made by Michael Traynor, a graduate of Loyalist College's wine program. Traynor also manages several vineyards in Prince Edward County.

Quai du Vin Estate Winery

To the southwest of Toronto are a few more wineries. Quai du Vin Estate Winery, located southeast of St. Thomas and about six miles (10 kilometres) from Lake Erie, has been open since 1989 and produces 6,500 cases of wine a year. Winemaker Jamie Quai, a

WINERY AND GARDEN

graduate of Brock University's oenology and viticulture program, points out that Quai du Vin has sold more than a million and a half bottles since opening. His parents, Roberto and Lisa Quai, first planted vines in 1971, and the vineyard now covers 24 acres (10 hectares). It's located in heavy clay on rolling hills north of the ridge of the St. Thomas Moraine, the region's highest point. The elevation provides good air movement, and Quai says the vineyard doesn't get the extreme cold that played havoc with vines elsewhere in Ontario from 2002 to 2005.

Labrusca varieties (including Concord and Niagara, which were among the first plantings), hybrids (including Vidal and De Chaunac), and vinifera (such as Riesling, Chardonnay, and Merlot) share the vineyard. Quai du Vin thus offers a rare opportunity to taste some wines made from labrusca and less-known hybrids, in addition to mainstream hybrid and vinifera varietals.

This is a family winery. Roberto and Lisa Quai run it, but their children, Jamie (the winemaker), Ryan (vineyard manger), and Dan and Lena (who contribute to various aspects of production and sales) are all engaged in the enterprise. The winery's underlying philosophy is that "a quality bottle of Ontario-grown, produced, and cellared wine doesn't have to be expensive," says Jamie Quai. Apart from their Vidal Gold icewine, Quai du Vin's wines sell between $7 and $14.

Thirty Three Vines

Farther east, several wineries are opening just outside Prince Edward County. They see themselves as "the gateway to Prince Edward County" for people coming to the County from the direction of Kingston. One is Thirty Three Vines, located on Highway 33 (Loyalist Highway) about ten kilometres east of the Glenora ferry, which links Prince Edward County to the mainland. The five-acre (two-hectare) vineyard is owned by Paul and Marilyn Minaker, who planted Riesling, Chardonnay, Pinot Noir, and Cabernet Franc in 2004. They have a slightly elevated lakeside location with a heavy clay base that they expect to do well during dry summers.

Paul Minaker is a telecommunications engineer who grew up in Picton, and he and Marilyn, an Ottawa school teacher, have had a cottage there for years. They've built a winery in a 100-year-old barn on their vineyard site and plan to pick a first crop in 2006 and to begin selling white wines in 2007. Asked what he aims at in terms of production, Paul Minaker says, "Well, I used to say about 2,000 cases, but now I'm thinking more of 4,000. It's still not a lot. We're going to be small."

There's no such thing as a typical Ontario winery. They come in all sizes, with owners and winemakers with different backgrounds and varying ambitions. They work in climatic and market conditions that are often challenging. But all exude the same passion for their work and their wines that will ensure that people will be drawn to Ontario wine country.

ONE-YEAR-OLD VINES AND ESCARPMENT

THE WINERIES

Cilento Wines
672 Chrislea Road
Woodbridge, ON L4L 8K9
Tel: 905-264-9463
www.cilento.com

Quai du Vin Estate Winery
45811 Fruitridge Line
St. Thomas, ON N5P 3S9
Tel: 519-775-2216
www.quaiduvin.com

Southbrook Winery
1061 Major Mackenzie Drive
Richmond Hill, ON L6A 3P2
Tel: 905-832-2548
www.southbrook.com

Thirty Three Vines
9261 Highway 33
Conway, ON K0K 2T0
Tel: 613-373-1133
www.33vines.com

Vinoteca Winery
527 Jevlan Drive
Woodbridge, ON L4L 8W1
Tel: 905-856-5700
www.toronto.com/vinoteca

Willow Springs Winery
5572 Bethesda Road
Stouffville, ON L4A 7X3
Tel: 905-642-9463
www.willowspringswinery.ca